Building Your Spiritual Palace

Rev. Dr. Timothy Ehrlich

Parson's Porch Books

www.parsonsporchbooks.com

Building Your Spiritual Palace

ISBN: Softcover 978-2-949888-96-6

Copyright © 2019 by Timothy Ehrlich

All rights reserved. No part of this book may be reproduced or transmitted in any form or by any means, electronic or mechanical, including photocopying, recording, or by any information storage and retrieval system, without permission in writing from the publisher.

Building Your Spiritual Palace

Contents

Foreword 7

About Me 11

A Note About Footnotes 13

Chapter One: A Pre-construction Introduction 14

Chapter Two: Blueprints 30

Chapter Three: Building the Outer Wall 40

Chapter Four: The Courtyard 50

The Importance of Play 50

Chapter Five: Preparing the Ground 62

Chapter Six: Money is an Obstacle or a Tool 80

Chapter Seven: The Foundation 95

Chapter Eight: Bricks & Mortar 107

Chapter Nine: The Dining Room 127

Chapter Ten: The Throne Room 140

Chapter Eleven: The Living Room 152

Chapter Twelve: The Bedroom 160

Chapter Thirteen: The Kitchen 170

Chapter Fourteen: The Servants' Quarters 185

Chapter Fifteen: Spiritual Maintenance 199

Chapter Sixteen: The Balcony 213

Foreword

This book is written for every Christian whose faith life is stuck in neutral; for everyone whose faith life is plateaued, and especially for who for everyone who wants to reach for the higher levels of what is possible in relationship with God through Jesus Christ in the Holy Spirit.

This book is built on the premise that Christianity contains within its teachings a blueprint for living the longest, healthiest, happiest, wealthiest, fullest and most intelligent life possible, and that all comes to us by living in a close personal relationship with God through Jesus Christ. So this book draws out the scriptures from both the Old and New Testaments that point the way to building materials and steps needed to build a most excellent life-enhancing relationship with God.

Spiritual health is comprised of a mixture of knowledge, faith, and application, in the daily practice of Christianity that all together lead to the development of close personal relationship with God. Many scientific studies have demonstrated that improved mental, physical, and emotional health and wellbeing are wonderful side benefits to true spiritual health; and other studies have shown that tending well to our mental, physical, and emotional health contribute to our spiritual health. Because spiritual health is inextricably intertwined with physical, mental, and emotional health this book takes a holistic approach to spiritual development that will help the reader take full advantage of the wide range of blessings that come to a person who lives in a close personal relationship with God.

In his parable about the man sowing seeds (Matthew 13:3-23) Jesus mentions or implies five different levels of relationship with God. I have certainly seen these five levels in the congregations of churches I have served over the years. The lowest level, failing, is hearing the Word of God but ignoring it. This Jesus illustrates as being like seeds that get eaten by birds before they can even sprout. The next level, for the sake of argument I will call "below average," are people with shallow faith. Jesus illustrates this as seedlings in shallow soil that dry up in times of trouble. Those with average faith are the crowd, they believe but their practice of the faith is choked by the business of their lives, and Jesus illustrates this as seeds growing up among weeds. Those with above average and excellent faith he describes as seeds growing in good soil, the above average who yield a 30-fold increase, and the exceptional yielding a 100-fold increase.

Over my thirty-five years as a pastor I have seen many people in my worship services with a "drug" problem – someone drug them to church, and they have no faith or interest in being there. I've seen a number of others who come to church, jump in with both feet and seem like they will become exceptional members but then they jump back out equally quick for any number of shallow reasons. The majority of congregation members I've served are busy with daily life, work, children, age or health concerns, so that just being in church is a strain ("Getting three kids under ten to a 9:00 a.m. worship service is a major military operation!") and they come to be nourished and sustained for the struggle not necessarily to grow. Lastly there are the pillars of the church, those who are turned on to serving and relating to God. They are the 20% who do all the work and give 80% of the church's income. A surprising number of these pillars come for social or other reasons, but a fair number come not just to be fed but to grow spiritually and find ways to serve. We see examples of these five levels of relationship with God throughout scriptures and the teachings of Jesus. Jesus' ministry was towards people in all five of these groups; this book has a narrower focus of helping the reader move from average to exceptional.

Jesus said that, "a person is a fool to store up earthly wealth but not have *a rich relationship with God*" (Luke 12:21 NLT). A rich relationship with God is represented in this book by the term *spiritual palace*. The image of a spiritual palace is derived from Jesus parable of a strong relationship with God as being like a well-made house:

> "When someone comes to me, listens to my teaching, and then follows it. It is like a person building a house who digs deep and lays the foundation on solid rock. When the floodwaters rise and break against the house, it stands firm because it is well built" (Luke 6:47-48 NLT).

In studying that parable for a sermon I thought about the tiny stone houses from Jesus' day that I saw at the Capernaum archeological site in Israel. They were little one-room dwellings made of stone; most were built on top of rock. I thought, "If that is what Jesus meant by 'a house on a rock' I want to live in a palace!" If a house on the rock is a good relationship with God, then a rich relationship with God is much better: it is a spiritual palace compared to a house.

I am lucky and blessed because I am not just a salesman, I am a satisfied customer. I have poured over forty years of my life into building a rich relationship with God, and now I live in spiritual luxury. When I think about how I have grown spiritually over the years since I first gave my life to God at age seventeen, I am so grateful. I have gone from questioning to experiencing, from believing to seeing, and from trusting to knowing. Now I am daily renewed by the Spirit, daily surrounded by experiences of the richness of God's grace and the beauty and the treasures of a living a Spirit filled life. I have a close personal relationship with God the Father, Christ the Son and the Holy Spirit. I have a wonderful assurance that I am intimately known by God and (undeservedly) deeply loved by God.

If you can say that about yourself and your relationship with God then I rejoice with you; if you cannot, then when are you going to do something about it? If you are content with your spirituality to be in the same place in five years as it is now, and as it was five years ago then this book is not for you. But if you want to grow continually, and reach your highest potentials then this book will offer lots of Biblically informed advice and lift up some of the wisdom of sages from all walks of life that together can be used as a relatively detailed blueprint or set of instructions for building a spiritual palace personal relationship with God.

About Me

I haven't forgotten the opening of Rick Warren's wonderful book *The Purpose Driven Life*: this book is not about me. I have prayed repeatedly throughout the writing of this book, "Lord this is Your word for Your people; help me stay out of the way." But I do show up a lot in this book, so I want to share a little about myself, starting with my spiritual and secular qualifications to write a book about reaching your highest potentials as a Christian. First, the Holy Spirit has shown me to be qualified by anointing me for this task. Three times in my life I have been completely immersed by a baptism in the Holy Spirit; twice before becoming a pastor and once after. Twice since becoming a pastor the Holy Spirit has come just to rest inside me in great power for twenty-four hours or more, and several times the Holy Spirit has used me to bring miraculous healing through prayer and the laying on of hands. When the early Church was trying to make the determination about whether or not to admit non-Jews into the Christian church (as described in Chapter 15 of the Acts of the Apostles), the decision was made with the determining factor being that the non-Jewish believers had received the Holy Spirit. I take my many exceptional experiences of and with the Holy Spirit as evidence that I am qualified spiritually.

Secondly, I also have significant temporal qualifications. I have served three years as a student pastor and thirty-two years as a United Methodist Minister of congregations in upstate New York, eastern Pennsylvania and central Florida. Before that I obtained a bachelor's degree in liberal arts from SUNY Stony Brook, a Master of Divinity degree from Duke Divinity School; and while serving as a pastor, attained a Doctor of Ministry degree from Asbury Theological Seminary, focusing my doctoral research on spiritual experience in clergy.

Finally, my life as a Christian has taken me through a wide range of experiences that have taught me how to keep my focus on

God in the midst of daily life. I am blessed to have had an interesting and somewhat unusual background for a pastor in that I am a former US Marine scout sniper. I have also worked as a private eye in Hong Kong, and as a bouncer and bartender in a disco in New York. I have been married for 38 years, happily; and my wife Anna and I have raised three boys and a girl to wonderful adulthood. I have suffered through personal losses and grief and illness of loved ones: the lowest of lowest and the highest of highs. Through it all God has always been with me and I have poured my heart into continually growing in faith and improving as a Christian.

Theologically I am a moderately liberal conservative, a scientifically minded man of faith; an evangelical but not a fundamentalist. My theological education has helped me to learn a lot about God, and the many miracles I've experienced have helped me to know God personally (to the extent that a human mind can understand God's infinity, eternity, omnipresence, and other divine characteristics). I have tried to combine these two sources (knowledge and experience) into this book. My greatest joy as a pastor is seeing people who have been lukewarm believers for years suddenly catch the fire of the Holy Spirit through my ministry. Ecclesiastes 3:3 says, "There is a time to build up." My hope and prayer is that for you this is your time, and this book may be a help.

A Note About Footnotes

These chapters were originally written as sermons and not academic works so I don't always footnote my scientific facts, but any facts I mention that are not footnoted can be easily verified by a search on the internet.

Below the title of each chapter you will find a date the sermon the chapter was based on was preached. The date is noted because my sermons can be found on YouTube and if you are interested you can search for my name and the date you will find the sermon.

Chapter One: A Pre-construction Introduction

I like to start everything I do for God with a prayer so that everything I do is done with God, so I want to invite you to join me in this prayer.

> Lord Jesus, You are an enigma to us. We struggle to fully understand how You can be, "the son of God and son of man" and, "fully God and fully human," but we see in Your teachings and example what a perfect relationship with the Father looks like. You inspired us to seek the heights of what is possible when You called us your brothers and sisters, and when You told us if we believe in You, we will do the same works You do, and even greater works. Father, we pray that by the example of Jesus and by the indwelling of Your Holy Spirit You will pull us gently but firmly, higher and closer to You every day. All these things we pray in Jesus name.

Jesus told us, "a person is a fool to store up earthly wealth but not have a rich relationship with God" (Luke 12:21 NLT). There are only two other places in the Gospels where Jesus calls anyone a fool or foolish - those who don't build their house on a rock by listening to him (Matt. 7:26), and those who after his resurrection refuse to believe what the prophets wrote about him (Luke 24:25). In the parable of building a house on a solid rock, Jesus said that those who don't come to him, listen to his teaching, and then follow his teachings are fools. That is the most basic level of relationship with God as a Christian: come to Christ, listen to His teachings, and obey them.

I imagine that since you are reading this book right now you have come to Christ, listened to his teachings and are trying to obey them. Jesus would say that you are not a fool, but what would He say about the quality of your relationship with God? Do you have a rich relationship with God? After more than forty-five years of working on my relationship with God I have a pretty rich relationship with Him, but I am still scratching the surface of what is possible with an infinite God. I am walking on the same difficult path you are that leads in the direction of perfection. The best teachers are also life-long students and I am still learning, still working to overcome sin in my life and build up my relationship with God into something truly spectacular.

In Psalm 90 we read, "teach *us* to number our days, that we may apply *our* hearts unto wisdom (Psalms 90:12 KJV). Knowledge about how to build a rich relationship with God takes discernment and application of effort to obtain: application because the Bible contains lots of little nuggets of golden advice on how to improve our relationship with God, but they are scattered around. Even in the so-called *wisdom literature* (Job, Ecclesiastes, Proverbs and the Song of Solomon) advice on improving your relationship can be found in a verse here, five verses there, and much advice must be inferred from proverbs that don't even mention God. Jesus said we would be fools not to have a rich relationship with God, but there is not a single quote in the New Testament where you can find Jesus saying, "This is how to improve your relationship with God" or "this is what you must do to improve your relationship with God."

Discernment is required because you have to be able to "read between the lines" of scripture and to interpret the sometimes-hidden lessons in the actions, speeches, proverbs and parables. There is not a single quote in the New Testament where you can find Jesus saying, "This is how to improve your relationship with God" or "this is what you must do to improve your relationship with God." Application is required because the Bible contains lots of little nuggets of golden advice on how to improve our relationship with God, but they are scattered around throughout the Bible.

As someone who has spent forty years applying myself to studying the Bible, I can at least give you a leg up, a shortcut on your journey. The good news is that you don't have to be a biblical scholar to succeed, but you do have to have a heart for God, and you need to read the Bible. A heart for God means it must be your heart's desire to know God and know about God. When Jesus said, "when someone listens to my teachings" for us that only happens through reading the Bible. So it takes a combination of heart and application to seek the knowledge and education that become the foundation and building materials of our spiritual palace. I can't give you a heart for God, but I have taken many of Jesus teachings and assembled them into a format leading to logical conclusions about how to build up a relationship with God.

For example, Jesus' familiar parable of building a house on a rock is this:

> "When someone comes to me, listens to my teaching, and then follows it. It is like a person building a house who digs deep and lays the foundation on solid rock. When the floodwaters rise and break against the house, it stands firm because it is well built. But anyone who hears and doesn't obey is like a person who builds a house without a foundation. When the floods sweep down against that house, it will collapse into a heap of ruins." (Luke 6:47-49 NLT).

We can fairly easily interpret or read between these lines to conclude that building a house on a rock is a metaphor for building a solid relationship with God through Jesus; a relationship that will protect us when life throws disasters at us.

We do need to be cautious in our interpretations even of passages like this that seem obvious because to really fully, accurately "unpack" this passage or any teaching of Jesus you need to not just have read it, but you must also be familiar with every teaching and action of Jesus in the Gospels.

When we add the teachings from this passage to all that Jesus taught by His words and actions about relationship with God it is clear that Jesus is offering more for us than just building a spiritual house on a rock relationship with Him. The teachings of Christ provide a blueprint for taking our faith life far beyond the basic minimum of saving faith (faith that saves us into heaven) through building up our faith into a spiritual house that can shelter us from the storms of life, all the way up to spiritual luxury where the miraculous becomes a fairly common experience and the indwelling of the Holy Spirit is a daily occurrence. To come to Jesus, to listen to his teachings and obey them is the minimum that He wants for His followers. Jesus offers much more for us than just a simple - hear and obey, one room dwelling on a rock relationship with God – He offers us real spiritual wealth; not just treasure in heaven (Matt. 6:19-21), but the luxury of being in a personal relationship with God in this life; a relationship with the one who is "The Ultimate Source Of Power And Reality In The Universe" (David Watson), the "Being Than Which Nothing Greater Can Be Thought" (St. Anselm).

The richness Jesus offers us is the blessing of being both a child of God and a friend of God. In Proverbs 31 we read about someone who is living in a spiritual palace relationship with God:

> "She is clothed with strength and dignity, and she laughs without fear of the future. When she speaks, her words are wise, and she gives instructions with kindness" (Proverbs 31:25-26 NLT).

Strength, dignity, confidence about the future, kindness, and wisdom are all part of the fabric of a spiritual palace relationship with God. Those who live in a spiritual palace relationship have confidence about the future that comes from certainty in their belief in God. They have no doubts about the reality of God; they have assurance that they are known by and loved by God. They know that their prayers are heard by God, and they experience God as a loving father and friend, who is close to them now and who they trust will be with them at all times. As a result of all of these blessings a Christian is "alleluia from head to toe" (St. Augustine), as Jesus said, "I have said these things to you so that my joy may be in you, and that your joy may be complete" (John 15:11 NRSV). This kind of relationship with God is true spiritual luxury, and by the grace of God, Jesus is calling us to experience all the blessings of the faith we hold.

A close personal relationship with God seems like an unlikely miracle: why would the eternal, omnipotent, omniscient God who created everything and holds everything together by His amazing power and wisdom, care deeply about you or me? But as unlikely as it seems, it is true: God offers us a close spiritual palace relationship with Him, and truly we would be foolish not to take God up on an offer like that!

An important point to remember is that the construction process of building a spiritual palace does not have a completion point. We may quickly build enough of a spiritual structure to live in comfortably but there will always be more to build, more to expand through our ever-increasing experiences with God. So this book will not give you a finished product at the end, it will get you a good start in the right direction.

My personal testimonial is that relationship with God is an amazing and wonderful blessing and an incomparable joy. God has blessed my life in some amazing ways; in addition to the forty-five miracles I have also lived a lot of life. I have traveled around the world several times; I've been to over 40 countries;

been madly in love (and still am with my beautiful wife Anna), I've skied down double black diamond mountains, been in a cage with mountain lions, scuba dived on amazing shipwrecks, been in boxing matches and basically experienced everything this world has to offer. Easily the greatest thing I have ever experienced is the incomparable spiritual luxury and blessing of the love of God. Miracles are just the love of God being expressed through a miraculous event, which I have been lucky enough to have had several dozen times, usually but not always while in prayer.

Psalm 84:10 understates the joy: "A day in your courts is better than a thousand elsewhere." What can make you feel better about yourself than to know that the Eternal Creator of all things knows you and loves you and wants a relationship with you? A person living in that kind of close personal relationship with God is able to be filled with joy peace, love, and hope in any and every circumstance of their life, even in the face of death and disaster. In this rich relationship one also experiences being showered with spiritual gifts, so much so that minor miracles become fairly common (weekly or better) and major miracles become an expected occasional reality (once or twice a year).

I recently had an experience which is a good example of the blessings of living in a spiritual palace. My youngest son Timmy suffers from cyclic vomiting; that is a terrible ailment in which one begins throwing up and cannot stop, sometimes for many hours. It is caused in part by obsessive compulsive disorder and his schizophrenia as well as a reaction to the medicine he takes to stabilize his mental symptoms. During a recent bout he began throwing up at 9 a.m. on a Thursday. It continued unabated and his mom and I brought him to the emergency room at 1 p.m. Finally at 2 a.m. they were able to get it under control enough for him to fall asleep. But then the vomiting started again the next day at about three p.m. and lasted till 2 a.m. Saturday morning. Then it started up again Saturday in the late afternoon.

The continual vomiting is painful both in the damage it does to the esophagus from the stomach acid and bile, but also the muscles of the abdomen become filled with lactic acid from repeated the involuntary contractions. He also has a mild form of autism and when the pain hits him, he reverts emotionally to being like a boy so there is a lot of crying and moaning associated with the pain.

I was calm and peaceful the whole time as I kept him company through all this, though I lost a good deal of sleep, but by midnight on Saturday I was exhausted and needed some help from God. Putting my head against his shoulder and a hand on his head and another on his chest I began pray from Nehemiah 8:10 over and over again, "The joy of the Lord is my strength. The joy of the Lord is my strength. The joy of the Lord is my strength." I had already been in prayer for Timmy off and on for the whole three days but after just a short time of praying this prayer continually, less than half an hour, suddenly the joy of the Lord did hit me such that I began to laugh and giggle. I instantly was able to give God every worry and concern and fear completely, and so every time I would say, "the joy of the Lord is my strength," I would feel that joy bubbling up inside me and it would make me giggle. I could hear Timmy cry out in pain and I would pray, "The joy of the Lord is my strength" and I would feel such great trust in God and such resultant inner peace that I would giggle.

This was not a negative mocking giggle; this was a holy joy bubbling up inside me until I couldn't contain it giggle. Together with the giggles came peace and a feeling of assurance that my prayers were being heard – what a relief! What a blessing! At that same time, within about three minutes of me getting the holy giggles his vomiting stopped for good. He was able to go home from the hospital the next evening. So my spiritual palace is a relationship with God that brings an increase in knowledge of God through this kind of experiencing of God's love in action in, through and around my life.

All of us – every person I know suffers from some level of insecurity. Doubt over one's self-worth can be caused by many different factors in our past or present. The more secure you feel about your loving relationship with the Eternal Creator of All, the more secure you feel about yourself. Part of what God is offering us is healing for our emotions. When Jesus said that your spiritual house, properly built (on the rock of knowledge of and obedience to the teachings of Jesus), will protect you from the storms of life: he was talking about protection from the emotional damage caused by things like illness, loss of employment, death in the family etc. If you can be at peace and even experiencing joy in the midst of a crisis, then you are not just in a house on a rock, you are living in a spiritual palace relationship with God.

Because building a spiritual palace also includes actively practicing the Christian faith with excellence in all areas of your life, the spiritual building process also delivers an extra measure of healthiness to your body, mind, and emotions. In researching for sermons over the years my Google searches for "is being a Christian good for your health?" have led me to read dozens of medical and psychological studies showing that Christians who actively practice their faith enjoy less depression, lower blood pressure, quicker recovery from surgery, longer life and other benefits as well.

Psalm 46 calls God, "a very present help in times of trouble," and Psalm 91 presents a high level of God's interactions with us:

> **Psalms 91:1-4 (NLT)** Those who live in the shelter of the Most High will find rest in the shadow of the Almighty.
> 2 This I declare about the LORD:
>   He alone is my refuge, my place of safety;
>   he is my God, and I trust him.
> 3 For he will rescue you from every trap

> <u>and protect you</u> from deadly disease…
> <u>His faithful promises are your armor and protection.</u>
> You will not fear the terror of the night,
>   or the arrow that flies by day,
> 6 or the pestilence that stalks in darkness,
>   or the destruction that wastes at noonday.
> 7 A <u>thousand may fall at your side,</u>
>   <u>ten thousand at your right hand,</u>
>   <u>but it will not come near you</u>…
> 9 Because you have made the LORD your refuge,
>   the Most High your dwelling place,
> 10   <u>no evil shall befall you,</u>
>   <u>no scourge come near your tent.</u>
> 11 For <u>he will command his angels</u> concerning you
>   <u>to guard you</u> in all your ways.

This passage and many others (Psalms 46:1; 61:2-3; 71:3; 121:7 to name a few) say that God is our protector and is always ready to help those who trust in God in their times of trouble. These passages and a number of others like it make it sound like our spiritual palace relationship with God comes with a built-in angel security force that is on standby 24 hours a day protecting us from all evil. While millions of Christians have on occasion experienced God intervening in some way on their behalf, the reality is that even in the best and closest of relationships with God our physical protection is not guaranteed 100%; and this 'less than complete' protection is God's plan and design.

If we have prayed about something and it does not turn out as we thought it should, if we have not been protected from some evil or scourge, we should not feel guilty or think, "if only I was a better Christian,'" or "if only we prayed more or had more faith it would have happened." It is certainly possible that we didn't pray and if we had it might have changed things, but sometimes God's will or plan is in another direction that we don't see or understand. I have done whole sermons on 'why we don't always get what we pray for.' There are about ten good reasons, ten things we either do, think or don't do that we should do that all result in failed prayer, but I am not going to go into all of that now. I will tell you that sometimes, quite often in fact we don't get what we are asking for and it has nothing to do with what we do or don't do, it is about what the will of God is.

God desires and requires us to have faith, and so in almost all of his interactions with us God always leaves room for faith. At the time that a miracle occurs the recipient has no doubt that this is the result of God. But God intentionally is so subtle and restrained in his ways that months later doubt can set in. God leaves room for our doubts because without doubt there is no need for faith. This is a complex and deep theological question that also takes in the question– "Why do bad things happen to good people?"

The realism of Ecclesiastes speaks to this very subject:

> **Ecclesiastes 9:11-12 (NRSV)** Again I saw that under the sun the race is not to the swift, nor the battle to the strong, nor bread to the wise, nor riches to the intelligent, nor favor to the skillful; but time and chance happen to them all. 12For no one can anticipate the time of disaster. Like fish taken in a cruel net, and like birds caught in a snare, so mortals are snared at a time of calamity, when it suddenly falls upon them.

These two passages, from Psalm 91 and Ecclesiastes 9, provide a good example of why you need to be familiar with every part of the Bible before you can speak authoritatively about what God wants or thinks about a subject. Ecclesiastes' version of God's protection is very different than that of Psalm 91. When the entire Bible is considered, the answer that emerges is a sort of hybrid or combination of both: it is in God's power to protect and save miraculously (as we see in the resurrection), but it is not always part of God's plan to do so, even for those He loves (as we see in the crucifixion). We must recognize the Biblical reality that while God is the ultimate power of the universe God's will is that, "the race is not always to the swift… but time and chance happen to all people."

Here is what I have learned from being a recipient of and participant in about four dozen miracles. God has a two-part rule about God's self-revelation: first, if we seek with all of our heart to know the reality of God, God will provide more than enough signs and proofs of His presence and reality to enable us to feel confident and assured about our faith. But second, God will not give us so many signs and proofs of His presence and reality to take away our need for faith. God's miracles are exceptions to His rule because they provide proof of the reality of God or leave little to no room for doubt that a supernatural intelligent caring force has been at work. That experience then takes away or reduces our need for faith, so God keeps miracles to a minimum to allow us to have to the maximum amount of faith. Even those of us who have had many demonstrations of His power still find a need to have faith and to trust in His ability and willingness to be our strength and protection.

Miracles are given to suit God's purposes, which often include blessing us, but the reasons for them (God's purposes or plans) are not always clear to us. I have several times seen a person receive a miracle that I would have thought undeserving, while others I think are far more deserving don't get a miracle even though I have prayed and asked God for a miracle for them.

To put this complex relationship that God offers us in simple terms: Jesus didn't say, "If you believe in me, I will make everything in your life all right," what he said was, "I will be with you always." (Matthew 28:20). Faith in and obedience to Jesus is not an iron clad guarantee of protection in every situation, but a) it dramatically increases your chances of being on the receiving end of a miracle; b) it dramatically increases your odds of healthiness, success and longevity; and c) it unquestionably gives you dramatically more peace, wisdom and protection as you are going through the storms of life. Following Jesus' rules for living will also protect you from making the kind of moral and ethical mistakes that can ruin your life. The result is that in several ways, active Christianity, and working towards building a spiritual palace is wisdom and good judgment personified.

The last question I want to answer in this lengthy introduction is about what you need get started in building a spiritual palace – **do you have what it takes?**

The main thing you need if you are going to build a spiritual palace relationship is commitment: "want to." There is a difference between being a believer in Jesus and being a disciple of Jesus; and again there is a difference between a disciple and an apostle. All three (believer, disciple & apostle) accept faith in Christ, confess that faith with his or her mouth, and believe in their heart that Jesus is Lord; and that Christ's sacrificial self-offering on the cross was sufficient offering for their sins. But the disciple goes beyond the ordinary believer to also committing to obeying Jesus' commandment to love God with all of his or her heart, mind, soul and strength, and to making a commitment to fully obey Jesus' teachings in all things.

The disciple is also a life-long learner committed to continually growing in knowledge and experience of God and becoming more and more obedient. No one can live at the top of the mountain of God, the air is too thin, but the Apostle has been to the mountain top and now lives in a spiritual palace at the base camp, like a spiritual Sherpa he or she is there to help other reach the summit as well. Really what all this boils down to is the believer has the minimal relationship with God, the disciple makes a commitment to have the best possible relationship with God, and the apostle has the best possible relationship with

God. The difference between them is the degree of want to, application, and persistence.

What Do We Need to Commit to?

Pastor Rod W. Larkins spoke to how we obtain the benefits of relationship with God:

> "God does not bless you because you're good, because you help others, because you give money, because you witness, because you come to church or any other overt activity... It is your eternal relationship with God that brings you blessing, not your personality or ability."

The eternal relationship Larkins mentions comes to us because we are committed to having one. Making a commitment to obeying Jesus' teachings starts us on the road to a lifetime of having a rich relationship with God. A commitment to obedience is the completion of the basic level of Christianity. Jesus calls us to in his parable about building a house on the rock, in it He says the wise person will: a) come to Jesus, b) listen to his teachings, and c) obey them.

The Bible gives us a simple set of things we need to do to be obedient. In the Old Testament, in the book of the prophet Micah we read: "what does the LORD require of you but to do justice, and to love kindness, and to walk humbly with your God?" And in the New Testament Jesus told us that there are two great commandments which sum up all of the laws and requirements of the Old Testament: to love God with all of your heart, mind, soul and strength; and, to love your neighbor as yourself (Matt. 22:37-40). The commitment to doing these things is the agreement that a disciple makes with God. In the Bible the agreement we make with God, to believe in Jesus and to try to follow his commandments is called entering into a covenant with God. Basically a covenant is a holy agreement with God. Our part of the covenant is to listen, believe, and obey; God's part is to bless us and protect us.

Our commitment to do justice, to love kindness, and to walk humbly with our God, and to obey Jesus' two greatest commandments qualifies us as disciples and starts us on the road to building a spiritual palace. If you have made that commitment it is something to celebrate. Paul writes: "now we can rejoice in our wonderful new relationship with God because our Lord Jesus Christ has made us friends of God" (Romans 5:11 NLT). Exploring and developing our friendship relationship with God, expanding it, and bringing it to the heights of what is possible makes life a joyous exciting adventure and that is what building a spiritual palace is all about.

Here is what I can guarantee you: everyone I have known who has committed him or herself to the task of building the best possible relationship with God (and I have known hundreds), says it is the best decision they made in their life. Committing your life to relationship with God sounds like a huge commitment, and it is huge to be willing to give every part of your life to God, every part of your heart, to hold nothing back from God. But ask anyone who has made that choice and they will tell you it's the best decision they've ever made and that it will lead you to blessing after blessing, and you will never regret it. At the very end of this chapter I have written a prayer you can use to make a commitment or a recommitment to God to be a true disciple.

One last point about making a commitment to God to construct a spiritual palace relationship: it may come with a cost to you. Jesus warned us (Luke 14:28-30 NLT), "But don't begin until you count the cost. For who would begin construction of a building without first calculating the cost to see if there is enough money to finish it?" The cost of committing yourself to the task of building the best possible relationship with God could be actually monetary, as your growing relationship with

God might make you realize that your current job is inconsistent with Jesus teachings, or you might realize you need to give far more than you currently give. The cost could also be in relationships. Jesus said:

> "I did not come to bring peace, but a sword. I came to set sons against their fathers, daughters against their mothers, daughters-in-law against their mothers-in-law; your worst enemies will be the members of your own family." (Matthew 10:34-36 TEV)

The price in relationships can be that as you grow and change and live into your commitment to be a disciple, others you have known all your life may not be happy with the new you; it happened to me. They will try to relate with you as you used to be and as they think you should still be and when you refuse to relate with them on that level they may try to mock you or pressure you into a retreat or they may just drop contact with you. Both of these highly likely possibilities are painful. You can only invite your family and friends to build palaces of their own, but not everybody will accept this invitation. While husband and wife live under the same physical roof, they may both also live in spiritual palaces, or one may live in a spiritual palace and the other in a spiritual shack, or even be homeless (have no faith at all).

Now the bottom line of this introduction is that basic Christian faith, and salvation into eternal life, are just the beginning. God offers us and God desires for us that we build up a rich relationship with God, a spiritual palace that has many beautiful rooms to explore and enjoy, a relationship that brings physical, mental, emotional and spiritual blessing after blessing into your life through a luxurious relationship with God. The requirement to have this kind of wonderful relationship with God is commitment to fully live out the three requirements given by Micah and the two commandments given by Jesus. If you are already on this path, that is wonderful for you! If you have not already made that commitment and would like to then please join me in this prayer:

> Lord God, You are good and great: all powerful all knowing, yet so loving. You temper Your justice with mercy and kindness for all who seek to walk humbly with You. Father, I commit to You now (again) that I will give my all to You to becoming a disciple of Your son Jesus, with all that means. I enter into this agreement with You with all my heart. Confirm this agreement, receive me as Your own and give me Your guidance and protection as I seek to walk Your path each and every day. In Jesus' name I pray.

Questions for Self-Reflection

- Can I say that I have a "house built on the rock" type of faith?

- Would I describe myself as being a believer, a disciple or an apostle?

- Do I have a rich relationship with God?

- Have I made a covenant with God to do justice, to love kindness, and to walk humbly with God, and to obey Jesus' two greatest commandments?

Chapter Two: Blueprints

Originally preached January 20, 2019

In Proverbs we read: "A house is built by wisdom and becomes strong through good sense. Through knowledge its rooms are filled with all sorts of precious riches and valuables" (Proverbs 24:3-4 NLT). Wisdom and good sense will also be needed to build our spiritual home into a spiritual palace. Part of the wisdom we need to build a spiritual palace is that if we are going to be successful in building a spiritual palace, we need to have in our mind a clear vision or strong concept about what the finished product will look like. If you can envision yourself building that palace, if you can picture yourself living inside it then that vision will help pull you forward motivating you towards completion. If you are not already in a place spiritually where you can visualize yourself in that kind of relationship with God, then when you finish this chapter I will offer you a prayer you can use to help you ask God to give you that vision.

A shack can be built with just an idea in the mind, no blueprints are required, but the bigger and more complex the structure you want to build the more detailed the plans you will need to construct it. However, before we go farther, let's join together for a prayer;

> Father I thank You for this book and the time to read and work in it today. I pray that all that the thoughts I have in response to this chapter would be acceptable in Your sight for You are my Father creator, my Savior Redeemer, and my Sustainer Holy Spirit.

At St. Andrew's, the church I served in Brandon Florida, I was one of its three pastors and one of my jobs was to be the staff liaison to the building committee. This was an important job because in the seven years I was appointed there the building committee led four major construction projects: two huge renovations and two construction projects of palace-sized million-dollar buildings. Among other things, I learned how important a detailed set of plans or construction blueprints is for the building project. Detailed construction blueprints for a building give detailed instructions, not just from the foundation up, but starting underground from the edges of the property, showing where every sewage and water line and electrical line will be. Before the ground is broken and long before the concrete is poured for the foundation the blueprints outline the exact location, orientation and dimensions of the building. A detailed plan for a palace sized building is huge. One of the buildings at the church I am now serving is 14,000 square feet, and its detailed construction blueprints are on three large, thick rolls of 2' X 3' sheets of paper that together weigh about twenty pounds!

Fortunately in building your spiritual palace you don't need a complete a set of detailed plans before you begin, but you do need to start with a vision, or a picture in your mind of what kind of relationship you want to have with God. Once you begin you find that the vision of your spiritual palace gets clearer and more detailed as you build. The vision is built up over time by reading & studying the Bible and other spiritual books, by praying, attending worship, and through Christian conversation. Some people find it helpful to summarize their vision in a brief written statement that describes their initial vision in a few words.

The practice of forming a vision statement is a well-known process among businesses as well as churches; almost all of the biggest businesses believe it is important to have a short vision statement that every one of their employees knows by heart to make sure all employees understand what the company stands for or is hoping to become. Apple, Microsoft and Netflix for example all have both a vision statement and a mission statement. I have attended a number of seminars and classes devoted to explaining why it is important for a church to have a vision statement and how to form one, and I have often heard Proverbs 29:18 (KJV) quoted, "Where there is no vision the people perish." In church, which is a spiritual business, we know that a vision is more than just a picture of what we hope to do or become or accomplish in the future. We know that a vision is also or can be an inspiration from God, a God-given picture of what God would like us to do or become or accomplish.

As Christians we understand that God gave us a picture of what a truly excellent relationship with God looks like in Jesus Christ. As disciples we work to implement that vision to make it a reality in our lives. As disciples we recognize that this vision is not as much our vision of what we want to accomplish as it is a picture of what God wants to happen in us The more years we spend in relationship with Christ the more important it becomes to us that we seek to live out God's vision for us.

If you are going to form a vision statement that clearly tells what God is calling you to do in your relationship with God, then I would endorse what experts I have read say about a vision statement: it should be expressed in seven words or less. It is challenging and may be difficult to shrink down the essence of what you want to accomplish for God into seven words or less, but it makes it easy to remember, and a vision statement that is not remembered is not of any use at all.

My vision statement is: "***Loving God, Loving Others, Loving Life.***" I chose it because it summarizes in seven words what Jesus said are the two greatest commandments: "You must love the Lord your God with all your heart, all your mind, all your soul and all your strength, and love your neighbor as yourself" (Mark 12:28-31). You could say that Jesus' two great commandments ("Love the Lord your God with all your heart, mind, soul, and strength, and, love your neighbor as yourself" Matthew 22:37-40) are God's vision statement for all of us. Whether you decide to have a vision statement or not, what is most important is that you have a clear picture in your mind of what your spiritual palace relationship with God will look like.

Maybe you are in a place where you are feeling that right now things in your life are too hectic, or too chaotic, too busy, or too demanding for you to concentrate on improving your relationship with God. If that is true for you then I hope and pray that someday soon things are better in your life! In the meantime author Brian Tracy speaks to that situation, "goals are the fuel in the furnace of achievement" so set a goal for yourself. The trick for us in moving our "someday" statements into "today" statements is setting actual goals for ourselves based on a clear vision of what it will look like when we accomplish what we want to accomplish.

W.C. Fields once said, "Remember, a dead fish can float downstream, but it takes a live one to swim upstream." Unfortunately, it's a sad truth that far too many people take a dead fish approach to their relationship with God: they are willing to go with the flow; they don't set any important goals for their relationship with God. They are content to go with the flow and "whatever happens, happens," and as a result, the only goal they set is to do just enough to "get by" or to keep things the same.

Yogi Berra once said, "If you don't know where you are going, you'll end up someplace else." That is ironically true in our spiritual life. What if you want to build a relationship with God, and you have the time, and things are not too hectic in your life, but you still cannot envision yourself building a perfect relationship with God? There are three possible causes to such a blockage. The most likely blockage is simply lack of time invested. Reading this book will help, as will taking time to pray (it may take hours of prayer to develop a vision). If you have not gotten unstuck after reading this book and after time in prayer then there may be a subconscious cause to your blockage: you may be feeling at some deep level unworthy due to some past sin or negative messages about yourself that you received as a child. In this case you would benefit from speaking with a pastor. Lastly there is small percent of chance that you are suffering from a blockage due to spiritual oppression.

Just as there is a Holy Spirit there is an unholy spirit. Sometimes good people unintentionally invite or allow evil to have a foothold in their mind or heart usually through unresolved anger or hatred, and this oppression shows up in continual negative thoughts, or fears about the future, or inability to pray. A pastor or strongly Christian brother or sister can help you grow past oppression through counseling, prayer and the laying on of hands. Lastly, you may at this time have only a weak or hazy vision of yourself in perfect relationship with God, but you do want to go for "a lot better than what I have now." Maybe you can say "I can't really picture it, but I will know what it feels like when I feel it. What matters the most is to set a goal of a rich relationship with God and commit yourself to reaching the goal.

Goals are about shooting for a target and hopefully eventually hitting it. If you have ever shot an arrow from a bow then you probably know that when you hold the bow level and shoot it the arrow will go a certain distance before gravity pulls it to the ground, but if you pull the bow back the same exact distance and aim higher the arrow can travel up to three times farther. The same is true in almost every part of life: if you aim higher you will go farther. Michelangelo the famous artist once wrote: "The greatest danger for most of us is not that our aim is too high and we miss it, but that it is too low, and we reach it." So aim high in your relationship with God.

The process of building a spiritual palace may take many years, maybe even decades before you can feel that you can say you have something you can be truly proud of in every way. A goal and a vision of yourself in that perfect relationship with God will help you stay strong when life happens. Some life events are so consuming that it takes years to work through them, things like a family member with a severe illness can demand so much from us that we have no mental energy to give to anything else at the end of the day. A vision that you keep in your heart and mind will allow you to step back into the work again later just where you left off, as the situations of your life allow it.

Don't be discouraged if building an excellent relationship with God takes a lot more time than you had hoped or expected. Joseph had to go through many years of slavery, and then prison and then service to Pharaoh before his destiny became clear. Moses waited 40 years in exile before the burning bush. Jesus knew of his destiny as a twelve-year-old and had to wait eighteen more years before beginning his ministry. My New Testament Professor Dr. Effird quoting Henry Wadsworth Longfellow once said to our class, "The mill of God grinds slowly but with infinite fineness." Our progress with God is God's hands and when it goes slowly it is because God does not want to force us to change. He is allowing our change to occur within us naturally as we are able to respond to His love for us. A vision is about setting a goal, but it is also about helping us stay on task to ensure long term success. If you can envision that spiritual palace and see yourself living in spiritual luxury inside it, then that vision will put you forward, motivating you towards completion.

I attended a seminar taught by Ezra Earl Jones, one of the authors of a book called *Quest for Quality in the Church*. He described the power of a vision like this: picture yourself standing on the banks of a fast moving, deep river say 40-50 yards across. The river is the circumstances of your life with all of its challenges and complications. On the opposite bank of the river is your goal, in our case the beautiful, gleaming spiritual palace relationship with God we want to build. Now a strong vision is like a rope tied to a tree on the other bank of the river. You can hold on to that vision and it will be like a rope as you cross the river of life filled with business and chaos, and your vision will keep you from being swept away from the spiritual palace and help you to pull yourself towards it.

The apostle Paul talked about how keeping a clear vision of the future will help you live a life that is pleasing God. In his letter to the Hebrews he said: "let us run with determination the race that lies before us. <u>Let us keep our eyes fixed on Jesus</u>, on whom our faith depends from beginning to end." And in his letter to the Philippians he wrote:

> "<u>I focus on this one thing</u>: Forgetting the past and <u>looking forward to what lies ahead</u>, I <u>run straight toward the goal</u> in order to win the prize, which is God's call through Christ Jesus to the life above." Philippians 3:12-13 (NLT)

Again in both of these passages we see the reality reflected that, having a clear vision of what we hope to accomplish with and for God helps us to push on through the race of life and attain that goal. So what is your vision? What is your blueprint for building a spiritual palace? Can you picture yourself having a perfect relationship with God? Can you picture serving God exactly how you want to serve and how God wants you to serve?

Through the prophet Jeremiah about 2700 years ago God said to the people of Israel words that are still true for the people of God today: "I know the plans I have for you," says the LORD. "They are plans for good and not for disaster, to give you a future and a hope." God has a vision, a plan, a hope and a desire for every one of us. God sees us as we are and as we could be if we would only yield every part of our lives to Him. In His grace God is continually, gently tugging on our hearts and prodding our minds calling us deeper and deeper, higher and higher and higher in relationship with Him. His grace together with our vision of who we can be in God and what we can do with and for God gently and continually pulls us forward and closer to God.

What you will find as you commit to your goal of excellence in your relationship with God is that God will reveal His plans for you one step at a time as you are ready to progress. Our part of visualizing and claiming the vision is simply to commit to ourselves in our heart and mind and commit with our mouth in prayer that we will build an excellent relationship with God through Christ. Jesus said, "the gate is narrow, and the road is hard that leads to life, and there are few who find it." Once you have committed to walking the narrow road of God, then all you need to do is make yourself available because God will continually pull on your heart and show you step by step what comes next on His road as you open your heart to Him.

So if you have committed to walk on God's narrow road, and if you have committed to God to build a spiritual palace, the next steps in your construction are to put up a construction wall, prepare the ground and foundation, and assemble the basic materials need for construction. Here is a prayer of commitment you can use before proceeding:

> Lord God, I thank You for Your love for me which was in place before the world began. I thank You, and give You all praise, honor, glory, and love, that in Your love and in Your grace, You are calling me into an ever closer, personal, loving relationship with You! Give me Father, the passion for You, the integrity of character, the compassion for others, the patience and persistence, the wisdom and discernment I will need to complete this journey and build a spiritual palace for You and for me. Strengthen in me a continually clearer vision of what being in a perfect relationship with You looks like. Help me Father to base myself in Your Holy Spirit and surround me with Your Holy Spirit so that I am protected from going in any wrong directions physically or mentally. Fill me with Your Holy Spirit so that I have the light and joy of God in me, for your joy is my strength. Cover me with Your

Holy Spirit to protect me from anyone or thing that would cause me harm. Thank You, Lord! In Jesus name I pray. Amen.

Questions for Self-Reflection

Do I trust that God has a vision for my life and what God would like to see in my life?

If so, have I shared that with another Christian to get their thoughts?

If not, what do I need to do to see more clearly God's vision for my life?

Do I have a clear vision for what a "spiritual palace" relationship with God would look like for me?

If not, what do I still need to do to acquire a vision for what God is calling me to do?

If so, have I made a vision statement that encapsulates what I feel God is calling me to do?

Scripture Quotes & Sermon Notes
Building Your Spiritual Palace: Part One - Blueprints 1/ 20/ 2019

Proverbs 29:18 (KJV) [18]Where *there is* no vision, the people perish: but he that keepeth the law, happy *is* he.

Hebrews 12:1-2 (TEV) [1]As for us, we have this large crowd of witnesses around us. So then, let us rid ourselves of everything that gets in the way, and of the sin which holds on to us so tightly, and let us run with determination the race that lies before us. [2]Let us keep our eyes fixed on Jesus, on whom our faith depends from beginning to end. He did not give up because of the cross! On the contrary, because of the joy that was waiting for him, he thought nothing of the disgrace of dying on the cross, and he is now seated at the right side of God's throne.

Philippians 3:12-13 (NLT) [12]I don't mean to say that I have already achieved these things or that I have already reached perfection. But I press on to possess that perfection for which Christ Jesus first possessed me. [13]No, dear brothers and sisters, I have not achieved it, but I focus on this one thing: Forgetting the past and looking forward to what lies ahead, I run straight toward the goal in order to win the prize, which is God's call through Christ Jesus to the life above.

Jeremiah 29:11-13 (NRSV) [11]For surely, I know the plans I have for you, says the LORD, plans for your welfare and not for harm, to give you a future with hope. [12]Then when you call upon me and come and pray to me, I will hear you. [13]When you search for me, you will find me; if you seek me with all your heart,

Matthew 7:13-14 (NRSV) 13"Enter through the narrow gate; for the gate is wide and the road is easy that leads to destruction, and there are many who take it. 14For the gate is narrow, and the road is hard that leads to life, and there are few who find it.

Chapter Three: Building the Outer Wall

Originally preached January 6, 2019

In this chapter I am going to talk about the first thing we need to begin to build our palace – after we have a vision or concept of what we are going to build and have made a commitment to God to build a most excellent relationship with God: a construction fence, an outer barrier that will be our wall of protection around the construction while we are building our spiritual palace. During the construction of a large building, before the ground is ever broken, the first thing happens is that a construction wall or fence goes up. Walls around a construction site provide some security for the equipment and supplies being used from thieves and vandals. Spiritually, there are thieves also: many situations and people that would like to rob you of your joy; therefore, the first part of building our spiritual palace is the construction of a wall. Our wall will protect our faith and our joy as well as the palace we are building.

The Biblical story of Nehemiah serves as an excellent illustration of our need for a wall. Nehemiah was a 5th century Jewish leader, who was employed as the cupbearer to King Artaxerxes of Persia. Nehemiah learned of the sad condition of the city of Jerusalem – that it had still not been rebuilt 145 years after its destruction by the Babylonians (in 586 B.C.), and 75 years after King Darius allowed the Jews to return to Israel from their captivity. Nehemiah begged for and was given permission from the King to rebuild the city walls of Jerusalem. With the wall in ruins the people were dispirited, discouraged, defeated; the wall represented protection and security and a confident vision for the future. Nehemiah had the vision to rebuild and his vision was contagious, the Jewish leaders immediately joined him. Nehemiah knew that the people of Israel had enemies around them, enemies who would try to stop them from building the wall, mock them and threaten them while it was under construction, and would not be defeated even when it was completed. The reconstruction of Jerusalem's wall took place in such difficult circumstances that those who worked on the wall had to have spears and swords with them at all times (Nehemiah 4:17-18). Never-the-less, because of what it represented the wall had to go up.

As it was in Biblical times our construction will also need to be carried out in challenging and often difficult circumstances. For Nehemiah it was external enemies; for us it is the business of our daily life that often leaves us exhausted and with little time for building up our relationship with God. You will also find that when you set out to build your spiritual palace there will be people who try to stop you, who mock you, threaten you, and when it is complete, will try to tear it down. Your wall will help protect you from external threats, from inertia and from internal failings in morality and ethics. So I want to lift up to you the elements that contribute to a good wall.

First though, I need to clear something up: the term 'building a wall to protect yourself' has potentially negative connotations. Some people build an emotional or mental wall to hide or keep their feelings from the people who they are in relationship with. Some people put up a false front to hide from others who they really are. Let me be clear, the wall I am talking about is a positive and healthy thing, this is not an emotional barrier to keep feelings away. This is a spiritual wall, built in coordination with the Holy Spirit to protect you spiritually, and to set up healthy boundaries concerning what you will and will not accept from yourself and others.

Your spiritual wall is something that you will build with the coordination and help of God. The building blocks are our knowledge about God and God's will, and our intentions and desire to please God. God provides the cement that hold the construction in place which is the Holy Spirit. We provide the labor by daily inviting God, as we did in the closing prayer in the last chapter:

> "Help me Father to base myself in Your Holy Spirit and surround me with Your Holy Spirit so that I am protected from going in any wrong directions physically or mentally... Cover me with Your Holy Spirit to protect me from anyone or thing that would cause me harm."

God then holds in place a spiritual barrier against spiritual evil to protect your faith against every circumstance and situation that would rob you of your joy and peace.

I have led a blessed, and I am absolutely convinced, a supernaturally protected life. As a teen I was a constant rule breaker and risk taker – a real wild child. When I turned twenty, I became a US Marine infantryman, then a Scout Sniper; and after the Marines a bouncer and bartender in a disco, and a private eye in Hong Kong. I have lived much of my life on the edge of convention and at times so recklessly; I gave my guardian angel quite a workout! And yet I have repeatedly experienced God's hand of blessing and protection. God has been a wall of protection for me saving me physically from death or destruction on a half dozen occasions; and protecting my family, and my ministry from potentially self-destructive moral lapses. I am not going to go into any detail, but I can say that I definitely was not living an exemplary Christian life until I got the call to ministry, but God was always a wall of protection for me anyway. In recent years I have puzzled over that quite a bit, I wondered why God was so faithful to me, blessing me with protection and many miracles when I was not so faithful to Him.

The answer is important to all of us - my heart was right with God even if my actions were not. God sees us as a work in progress. God knows that the body and the mind will in time follow our heart. The prophet Jeremiah wrote words to God that are true for us as well, "But as for me, LORD, you know my heart. You see me and test my thoughts" (Jeremiah 12:3 NLT). God knows what is in our hearts, and it is pleasing to God when we set our hearts towards building a spiritual palace relationship with God: towards developing and growing our love for God, until we can truly say: "I love God with all my heart, soul, mind, and strength!" Paul writes: "it is by believing in your heart that you are made right with God" (Romans 10:10). So what is in our heart is what is most important to God. What God wants is that we have committed in our heart to know God, to love and obey God. That is good news for all of us because, isn't it a lot easier to love God than to obey God?

So I am saying that our faith can precede our faithfulness; our belief often precedes our obedience. God is a loving protective father because of our faith and our love for Him – not because of our obedience. God's acts of protection in my life have greatly increased my faith and thus my obedience. The apostle Peter wrote: "Through your faith, God is protecting you by His power" (1Peter 1:5 NLT); he did not write, "because of your obedience God is protecting you." The Bible tells us (Psalms 103): "The LORD is like a father to his children, tender and compassionate to those who fear him. For he knows how weak we are; he remembers we are only dust." Yes of course God wants us to obey Him and God has limits on His patience with us, but my experience, and my exhaustive reading of the scriptures tell me that God provides a wall of protection for us as soon as we commit in our hearts to Him. This is not just my experience; the people of God have experienced God's protection for millennia, that is one of the main reasons why there is still a church today.

The wall of Jerusalem is a good analogy of the kind of barrier God provides. In its current form the wall around Jerusalem is a beautiful 16th century renovation carried out by Sultan Suleiman the Magnificent in 1537. It gives the old city of

Jerusalem the appearance of a fortress. The wall of Jerusalem gives protection by its height and thickness, but it was also constructed to allow for an active defense, with probably a thousand slots to fire arrows through and many platforms to launch trebuchet from in its nearly 2-mile circumference. But a wall cannot fight; it cannot go on the offensive; without defenders it sits in passive, easily surmountable resistance. In the same way God provides a wall for us but we must man the parapets with the help of the Holy Spirit.

Jesus said that when we are facing trials because of our faith the Holy Spirit will help us find the right words to speak (Matt.10:18-20). The apostle Peter wrote: "Through your faith, God is protecting you by His power" (1Peter 1:5 NLT), and in the Psalms we read:

> The LORD says, "I will rescue those who love me. I will protect those who trust in my name. When they call on me, I will answer; I will be with them in trouble. I will rescue and honor them." Psalms 91:14-15 (NLT)

God is our protector. The wall is God's protection, but we must do our part through believing in Jesus and committing to obey him, and through daily opening our heart to, and inviting in the Holy Spirit.

Our commitment to obedience is a commitment to God to hold a set of Godly values and behaviors, that also define us as disciples. Construction of the wall, by holding to Godly values and behaviors, is an outward expression our love for God. This is not a transactional relationship where we adhere to a set of values and behaviors to gain protection; we adhere to a set of values and behaviors because we love God and have faith in God's love for us, and we desire to please Him. We love God in part because we respect and admire His power and abilities including the power to protect us, and we act in response to His love for us (1John 4:19), but not to leverage His power and abilities for our uses. In the same way, God uses His powers and abilities not to leverage our love (although our experience of God's protection and love for us does increase the amount of love we feel for God) but because He first loved us.

In simple terms ours is intended to be the simple relationship of love between a father and his children. John writes: "to all who believed him and accepted him, he (Jesus) gave the right to become children of God." A father doesn't love and protect his children to leverage their love; he acts in love regardless of whether his actions will even be known to his children, just because he loves them as a father. As His children God is our protector and defender because He is our loving father, and we love him for all the reasons that a child loves his or her father, which can include admiration and respect for his power and strength.

So then, what are the set of Godly values and behaviors we need to have as our part of building our wall? Jesus described the basic minimum as: coming to Him, listening to His teachings, and obeying Him. What do we obey? Jesus gave us two so called "great commandments;" that He said sum up all of the laws and commandments in the Old Testament (Matthew 22:40 TEV). His two essential commandments are: "to love the Lord your God with all of your heart, soul, mind, and strength; and to love your neighbor as yourself" (Mark 12:28-31 NLT). In case we had any doubts about what these commandments mean Paul added this clarification:

> The commandments, "Do not commit adultery; do not commit murder; do not steal; do not desire what belongs to someone else"—all these, and any others besides, are summed up in the one command, "Love your neighbor as you love yourself." 10If you love

others, you will never do them wrong; to love, then, is to obey the whole Law. Romans 13:9-10 (TEV)

If we are sincerely committed to obeying the two great commandments, then over time our values and behaviors will more and more reflect that love.

Proverbs 1:7 says, "The fear of the Lord is the beginning of knowledge." As long as your relationship with God is based simply on coming to Jesus, listening to his teachings and obeying Him, then it is not really based on love. At this basic beginning point, you don't really have a personal relationship with God. But over the years, as we build up our relationship with God through prayer and study and service, our values and behaviors will reflect more and more of our love of God and our love of others in his name. In time, as the number our experiences with God's grace grows then our faith grows, and our fence changes from a temporary construction fence we are only barely or occasionally aware of, into an awareness that you and God have built together something that not only protects you, but something you can admire and draw strength from and grow your faith from. In time you will say, "Look, God has been my wall of protection. Time and again he has shown that he loves me, and now I am blessed to be able to say truly that I also love God with all my heart, soul, mind, and strength!"

Once you have come to Jesus, listened to him, and have made a commitment to God to build a spiritual palace, your construction wall is in place and you are ready to build in earnest. So here is your inventory before beginning construction.

- Do you have a vision of what a "spiritual palace" relationship would look like and / or have you set it as a goal you are committed to?

- Have you come to Jesus (accepted Jesus Christ as Lord), listened to him (learned his commandments) and committed in your heart to obey him?

- Are you seeking to love God with all of your heart, soul, mind and strength?

Here then is a little prayer you can use before proceeding:

Lord God, I thank You for Your love for me which was in place before the world began. I thank You, and give You all praise honor glory and love, that in Your love and in Your grace, You have called me into a close, personal, loving relationship with You! Strengthen in me a continually sharper vision of what being in a perfect relationship with You looks like. Give me Father, the strength, the patience and persistence, the wisdom and discernment I will need to complete this journey for You and for me. Help me Father to base myself in Your Holy Spirit, surround me with Your Holy Spirit so that I am protected from going in any wrong directions physically or mentally. Fill me with Your Holy Spirit so that I have the light and joy of God in me, for Your joy is my strength. Cover me with Your Holy Spirit to protect me from anyone or thing that would cause me harm. In Jesus name I pray. Amen.

Scripture Verses for Chapter Three

Nehemiah 4:17-18 (NLT) The laborers carried on their work with one hand supporting their load and one hand holding a weapon. [18]All the builders had a sword belted to their side. The trumpeter stayed with me to sound the alarm.

Jeremiah 12:3 (NLT) But as for me, LORD, you know my heart. You see me and test my thoughts.

Romans 10:9-10 (NLT) 9If you confess with your mouth that Jesus is Lord and believe in your heart that God raised him from the dead, you will be saved. 10For <u>it is by believing in your heart that you are made right with God</u>, and it is by confessing with your mouth that you are saved.

1Peter 1:5 (NLT) Through your faith, God is protecting you by His power.

Psalms 103:13-14 (NLT) <u>The LORD is like a father </u>to his children, tender and compassionate to <u>those who fear him</u>. For he knows how weak we are; he remembers we are only dust.

Matthew 10:18-20 (NLT) You will stand trial before governors and kings because you are my followers. But this will be your opportunity to tell the rulers and other unbelievers about me. 19When you are arrested, don't worry about how to respond or what to say. God will give you the right words at the right time. 20For it is not you who will be speaking—it will be the Spirit of your Father speaking through you.

1 John 4:19 (NLT) We love each other because he loved us first.

Matthew 22:40 (NLT) The entire law and all the demands of the prophets are based on these two commandments."

Additional Verses (Not quoted but still relevant)

Psalms 33:12-21 (NLT) <u>What joy for</u> the nation whose God is the LORD, whose <u>people he has chosen as his inheritance</u>. The LORD looks down from heaven and sees the whole human race. From his throne he observes all who live on the earth. He made their hearts, so he understands everything they do. But <u>the LORD watches over those who fear him</u>, those who hope for his mercy. <u>He rescues them from death and keeps them alive in times of famine.</u>

Romans 10:9 (NRSV) If you confess with your lips that Jesus is Lord and believe in your heart that God raised him from the dead, you will be saved.

Proverbs 29:25 (NLT) [25] Fearing people is a dangerous trap, but trusting the LORD means safety.

Psalms 94:17-22 (TEV) [17] If the Lord had not helped me, I would have gone quickly to the land of silence. I said, "I am falling" but your constant love, O Lord, held me up... Whenever I am anxious and worried, you comfort me and make me glad... But the Lord defends me; my God protects me.

Luke 6:47-48 (NLT) I will show you what it's like when someone comes to me, listens to my teaching, and then follows it. 48It is like a person building a house who digs deep and lays the foundation on solid rock. When the floodwaters rise and break against the house, it stands firm because it is well built.

1 John 5:1 (NRSV) [1]Everyone who believes that Jesus is the Christ has been born of God, and everyone who loves the parent loves the child.

Chapter Four: The Courtyard
The Importance of Play

Originally preached February 10, 2019

This chapter is about a spiritual practice that begins pre-construction, but which should also continue on doing throughout the construction and when your construction is substantively complete. The spiritual practice I am talking about is making a space and time for play in your life, as a part of honoring God's commandment to take a day of rest. I am using the metaphor of constructing a courtyard for your palace with the idea that this is a play space. Of course you might just as easily conceive of a playroom inside, but I am placing outside because we haven't broken ground yet metaphorically speaking.

Would you join me in a prayer?

> Lord God, there is a lot to know about building a most excellent relationship with You; and it seems complex, so let us not lose sight of its simplicity. At its core all we are doing is expanding our love vocabulary, learning how to deepen our faith, to love You more and to be more filled with Your Holy Spirit. Help us to open our hearts to Your love, to open our minds to Your wisdom and open the totality of our being to Your Holy Spirit. Thank You Lord, in Jesus name we pray.

If we were constructing an actual physical palace the last thing to be completed would probably be the courtyard – in a typical construction the sod and the shrubs are generally the last things to go in. But just as we need a construction wall before we get into constructing a spiritual palace, in the same way we need to take care of our health, to stay healthy physically if we hope to complete it, and that is what the courtyard is all about–emotional and physical healthiness through play and rest.

When my son Timmy was a little kid, he thought it was the funniest thing ever, to ring our neighbors' doorbell then run and hide where they couldn't see him. He was a sneaky little guy too, I only found out about it when I discovered him hiding behind my car one day and asked him what he was doing. Kids love to play, and kids are mischievous, but Jesus said, "I tell you the truth, unless you turn from your sins and become like little children, you will never get into the Kingdom of Heaven" (Matt. 18:3 NLT).

Another example: when my oldest son Ian was five, I had put him to bed, and a few minutes later he started yelling for me. I quickly went to his bedroom. He was sitting up in bed and he said, "I am going to throw up." I said, "Well don't sit here go into the bathroom!" I will never forget it – he skipped from his room to the bathroom and immediately threw up. I thought - only a kid could have that much enjoyment of life to skip on his way to throwing up. So at least in the enjoyment of life and the love of play the traditional roles are reversed and children are our role models.

Spiritual growth is a serious subject so the idea that playing is important to spiritual growth might seem the opposite of what you might think about spiritual growth, but for a number of reasons, making time for play (not just for rest) as a part of your observation of the Sabbath is vital for nurturing a playful and humble spirit. Making time on a regular basis to engage in recreational activities is essential to your spiritual growth and healthiness. The Biblical foundation for this idea claim is found in the two great commandments. When Jesus said that the second great commandment is to, "love your neighbor *as you love yourself.*" That is sort of hidden commandment within that commandment: that we love ourselves. God expects us to love ourselves. Loving yourself in a Godly way, in a healthy and appropriate way, means that you are committed to taking the best possible care of the health of your body, your mind, your soul and your emotions.

It is a part of God's plan for each of us that we love ourselves appropriately: as children of God who are of sacred worth and great value. Unfortunately, many people fall short of loving themselves: even more than failing to honor the Sabbath day. The most frequently broken commandment is to love as Jesus told us to, followed immediately by failing to honor the Sabbath day. Jesus said; "The Sabbath was made to meet the needs of people, and not people to meet the requirements of the Sabbath." (Mark 2:27 NLT). As a pastor I work on Sunday. I worship, but leading worship and preaching is work, as is attending the meetings I frequently have on Sunday. So I break my Sabbath day of rest up into pieces. I believe the goal of God for us in establishing the Sabbath was that we honor God by using some time to rest and care for our physical needs and emotional needs, as a part of our obedience to God. So I worship on Sunday and take some time off on Monday and maybe an hour or two elsewhere in the week. The plan is that the total amount of time taken off in a week equals at least one Sabbath day.

We would be well advised to use the part of our time not spent on worship on the Sabbath day for vigorous physical activity. I say that because how many people do you know that need to take better care of themselves physically? I know many people like that, including myself, and you probably do too. And how many people do you know whose health would be better if they lost weight, or if they exercised more, or stopped smoking? Unfortunately many of us treat the incredible miraculous gift of our own body like that unwanted Christmas gift you got, and you threw in some forgotten corner.

God loves you deeply and because God loves you, if you fail to love yourself as you should, it is like you are challenging God or calling God's judgment into question. I know many people who love themselves a little bit, but they feel unworthy of being loved. I know other people who don't even like themselves let alone love themselves. There is an old saying, "Hate the sin but love the sinner;" have you heard that before? Unfortunately, when it comes to themselves, many people love their sin and hate the sinner: they hate something about themselves and that hate overshadows their feelings towards their whole person. I read something one pastor wrote about that: "Since Jesus Christ gave himself to die on the cross to get you forgiveness for all your sins, wouldn't it be wrong for you not to forgive yourself?" Lastly, I know so many people who love themselves but somehow don't find the time or will power to make sufficient time for taking care of themselves.

In the study I did for my doctoral dissertation I interviewed fourteen pastors who our Bishop nominated as the most successful pastors out of the more than 700 in the Florida Annual conference. And I also interviewed a number of other more typical pastors for comparison. I found that the most highly successful pastors all had six things in common that they all did, and one of those things is they all exercise at least twice a week. They all recognize the importance of both physical and emotional health and were diligent in caring for both. In fact, our commitment to healthiness physically and emotionally, to the extent that we can control our health, is a vital part of being able to build a spiritual palace, and that requires that we make time for play.

Jesus said: ""Healthy people don't need a doctor—sick people do. I have come to call not those who think they are righteous, but those who know they are sinners" (Mark 2:17). That is good news for those of us whose neglect of our physicality boarders on sin. To build a spiritual palace we must be committed to our health because our spirituality is inextricably attached to and influenced by our physical, mental, and emotional healthiness or the lack thereof. Our emotions are attached to our bodies and they have an interactive relationship: if you are unhealthy emotionally it tends to result in poorer physical health; if you are unhealthy physically it tends to result in poorer emotional health. If you are unhealthy mentally it generally results in poor physical health and emotional difficulties as well.

The apostle Paul said that your body is a temple of the Holy Spirit (1Corinthians 6:19). It's okay if the temple gets some snow on the roof (white hair), but if we don't take care of our "temple" to the point where the walls are falling in, then we are doing something wrong. Taking care of the temple means exercising physically, caring for our emotions, and mental health through having enough fun to stay healthy and balanced.

I have known several pastors who have gotten into trouble because they were so busy serving God that they forgot to do the most important part of serving God – taking the time to build their spiritual palace - keeping their relationship with God in top shape. One of the temptations or distractions I think we all face is getting so busy doing, working, accomplishing, and completing the tasks of our daily lives that we forget, or we neglect to take time to enjoy life, and have fun. George Bernard Shaw the famous Irish playwright put it this way: "We don't stop playing because we grow old; we grow old because we stop playing." I have a sneaking suspicion that if those pastors who got in trouble had ordered their lives enough to regularly play legitimately, they wouldn't have gotten into trouble for playing around illegitimately.

The Book of Ecclesiastes has more to say about the importance of having fun than any other book in the Bible. The author, who is believed to be King Solomon, famously said, "There is a time for laughing and a time for dancing," and he wrote:

> *I recommend having fun*, because there is nothing better for people in this world than to eat, drink, and enjoy life. That way they will experience some happiness

along with all the hard work God gives them under the sun. **(Ecclesiastes 3:12-13)**

Solomon must have really believed that to be true because in the twelve chapters of Ecclesiastes he tells us five times to enjoy life with food and drink. Please don't take this as a ringing endorsement for alcohol abuse. Rule one is take care of the temple – when in doubt refer to rule one.

I am often reminded when I read Ecclesiastes, of an old saying that: "people sacrifice their health to pile up wealth, and then they use their wealth to try and repair their health." The writer of Proverbs writes, "A cheerful heart is a good medicine" and we know that that is true: making time for play and recreation in our lives is healthy for us emotionally and physically. You have probably all heard that there are lots of studies that have shown that playing games like chess, or bridge or doing puzzles helps older people to fight dementia and Alzheimer's disease. Other studies have shown that making time each week for play helps you lower your blood pressure: and if you are a student, play breaks relax you and help you to do better in school.

When we play, we are only doing what comes naturally. One scientist, Dr. Marc Bekoff, in his book, "Animals at Play: Rules of the Game," showed that all kinds of animal's play including squirrels, mice, elephants, cats, dogs, bears, monkeys, sea lions, crows, coyotes, and kangaroos. Another scientist found, and this is disgusting, that even cockroaches like to play (I think their favorite game is "guess which human dropped this crumb"). So I guess when you flip on the light and the roaches all run away you may have just broken up a cockroach soccer game.

Have you ever been told to, "act your age not your shoe size!" Most of us have been told many times when we were growing up to be on our best behavior, or to act like a grown up. The tendency for most people is that as we get older, the playful child inside us gets buried, pushed down under the weight of responsibility, and so we need to be reminded to play more, at least most of us do. James A. Garfield, 20th president of the USA, wrote, "If wrinkles must be written upon our brows, let them not be written upon the heart. The spirit should never grow old." – it is play that keeps our hearts young. Imagine for a moment that Jesus is looking at the amount of play and recreation you are doing for your health. As Jesus is watching all you are doing, is he nodding and smiling or is he shaking his he

ad? Let me tell you, if he is slapping his forehead you have your work cut out for you!

The biggest issue that most of us have about making time for play in our lives is not that we don't want to play, but just finding time to do it consistently. One of the most effective tools that I have found that helped me figure out how to make time is in a book by Steven Covey, entitled *The Seven Habits of Highly Effective People*. What he suggests is to think about your week as a large glass bowl. Your week can only hold so many hours of activities. He said think about the things that are most critical to your health, wellbeing, and success as big rocks, and put them into the bowl first, or in other words put them into your calendar and let nothing but an absolute emergency take them back out. Then fill in the rest of the bowl, the rest of your weekly calendar with all the other little or less important stuff – let them be like sand and gravel pouring down around the big rocks; make the little things fit around the big rocks. Covey's observation is that if you don't put the big rocks in first the other stuff will fill in and the big rocks won't all fit. So my advice is - look at exercise and time for fun as the big rocks in your week. By the way when I stood at the door on Sunday morning after giving this advice, one of my parishioners said, "You know pastor – after the bowl is completely filled with sand and gravel and rocks you can still pour in a beer – so there must always be time for beer."

No matter how old we are we can still exercise, and no matter how busy we are we can make time for fun. Maybe your work requirements prevent you from taking a Sabbath day rest. You just need to be creative, two hours day, even in the middle of the day, for a walk, or a swim, or to read a book or take a nap seven days a week adds up to a Sabbath day. Make sure you treat yourself, as a person of sacred worth and great value, as a person whose physical and mental health is important to God.

So you need to make a place in your life for play, and by that, I mean carving out regular time in your life for play, so that you can stay healthy in your heart and mind and emotions, while you are building, and as part of building your spiritual palace. I compiled a list (below) of ten things you can do to help yourself stay young at heart.

Questions for Self-Reflection

- Am I committed to taking the best possible care of the health of my body, my mind, my soul and my emotions?

- What of these four areas of healthiness, if any, do I need to improve on? And why?

- Do I enjoy life? Why or why not? If not, what would I need to change to allow me to enjoy life?

- Do I make regular time in my life for play?

Scripture Quotes & Sermon Notes
Building Your Spiritual Palace Part Four:
The Courtyard – The Importance of Play
2/ 10/ 2019

Matthew 18:3 (NLT) ³Then he said, "I tell you the truth, unless you turn from your sins and become like little children, you will never get into the Kingdom of Heaven.

1 Corinthians 6:19 (NRSV) ¹⁹Or do you not know that your body is a temple⸤ of the Holy Spirit within you, which you have from God, and that you are not your own?

1 Thessalonians 4:6-8 (TMSG) <u>God</u> hasn't <u>invited us into</u> a disorderly, unkempt life but into <u>something holy and beautiful—as beautiful on the inside as the outside. If you disregard this advice</u>, you're not offending your neighbors; <u>you're rejecting God</u>, who is making you a gift of his Holy Spirit.

Ecclesiastes 3:1-4 (NRSV) 1For everything there is a season, and a time for every matter under heaven: a time to be born, and a time to die; a time to plant, and a time to pluck up what is planted; … a time to weep, and <u>a time to laugh</u>; a time to mourn, and a <u>time to dance</u>;

Ecclesiastes 3:11-13 (NLT) ¹¹Yet God has made everything beautiful for its own time. He has planted eternity in the human heart, but even so, people cannot see the whole scope of God's work from beginning to end. ¹²So I concluded <u>there is nothing better than to be happy and enjoy ourselves as long as we can.</u> ¹³And people <u>should eat and drink and enjoy the fruits of their labor, for these are gifts from God.</u>

Ecclesiastes 8:15 (NLT) <u>So I recommend having fun,</u> because there is nothing better for people in this world than to eat, drink, and enjoy life. That way they will experience some happiness along with all the hard work God gives them under the sun.

1 Corinthians 6:19 (NLT) Don't you realize that <u>your body is the temple of the Holy Spirit</u>, who lives in you and was given to you by God? You do not belong to yourself,

Luke 18:16-17 (NLT) Then Jesus called for the children and said to the disciples, "Let the children come to me. Don't stop them, for the Kingdom of God belongs to those who are like these children. 17<u>I tell you the truth, anyone who doesn't receive the Kingdom of God like a child will never enter it.</u>"

Proverbs 17:22 (NLT) A cheerful heart is a good medicine.

1 Timothy 4:8-9 (NLT) "<u>Physical training is good</u>, but training for godliness is much better, promising benefits in this life and in the life to come." 9This is a trustworthy saying, and everyone should accept it.

Ten Ideas for Keeping Your Heart Like a Child's

1. Since Jesus said, 'if we don't receive the Kingdom of God like a child, we will never enter it,' take some time to think about your attitude towards life and how open or closed your heart is. Ask God to help you have a childlike appreciation for life.

2. Go on an adventure, travel. Never stop traveling. Travel helps promote a healthy mind, and an open heart. Don't just sit around on your days of rest. Find something fun that you normally wouldn't do like visiting every Greek restaurant within 50 miles, or take a day trip on a charter fishing boat

3. Stay current; stay informed: keep up with current trends and news items. Listen to the radio stations you wouldn't normally, watch the news and read the papers. Use the Internet as an information tool. Buy new modern clothing.

4. Do things you would do if you were a kid: Go see a kid's movie; go to the aquarium, or a museum, or a nearby tourist attraction. If something looks interesting, take a break and go! Play a game you used to love or read a book you used to love.

5. Get excited over little things: take a walk through a park or at the beach or around the block and notice as many different things you can see, hear, smell and feel, and thank God for every different one.

6. Give yourself permission to be goofy: tell corny jokes, make a funny face, and hum a song while you are standing online in the grocery store. Don't be afraid to let your inner goofball out, Kids never worry if someone thinks they are weird; they just do what they want. So be as honest as a child, tell someone they are handsome or pretty or boring. If something gets you excited tell someone about it.

7. Do a hands-on art project. Finger paints, junk item sculpture, decoupage, or color in a coloring book with crayons.

8. Have a childlike optimistic attitude about life: kids forget about whatever just went wrong, and don't worry about the future.

9. Go to a restaurant and order off the kids' menu, or just order several deserts for dinner.

10. Keep exercising, it literally helps you stay young at heart. So put on some music and have your own dance party, and dance around like no one is watching. Regardless of your physical condition there is some form of exercise you can do.

Chapter Five: Preparing the Ground, The Importance of Self-Examination

Originally preached February 17, 2019

In this chapter we move at last to beginning construction in earnest – from making a commitment to taking action, and from understanding to implementation. Once we have a vision of what a spiritual palace relationship with God will look like for us (our blueprints), and the construction fence has gone up (we have made a commitment to God to seek excellence in our relationship with Him), then next phase in construction is preparing the ground for the foundation. By preparing the ground I mean preparing your heart and mind to truly be ready spiritually for the construction of your spiritual palace to begin. But before I go on to that I want to share a prayer with you.

> Lord God, I thank You for the awesome privilege and responsibility of being a disciple of Jesus Christ. It is a privilege to know that I am accepted as Your child through my faith in Jesus and my acceptance of His self-offering on the cross for my sins and the sins of the world. Lord, I offer myself to You unreservedly: my body, mind, soul, all I have and all I am, and I thank You Father both for the many joys I have already received and for those that I know are still before me as I continue in my relationship with You. Amen.

It occurs to me that at this point you may be thinking, "Hmm, I am five chapters into this book and this building a spiritual palace thing is more complicated than I thought. I am not so sure I want to do all of this." So I have a few words of encouragement for you: do you know how old Moses was when God came to him in the burning bush and sent him to Egypt to free the Jews from their slavery? He was 80. And how old was John when his gospels were written? The experts tell us he was around 90. How young was David when God called him into service? The Bible does not specify, it just tells us that he is a boy too small to wear a man's armor. And how young was Mary when the angel Gabriel announced to her that she would be the mother of Jesus? She also is believed to have been a teen. So my point is whether you are a teenager or in your nineties, there is no bad time to start, and the best time to start is right now. In fact there is probably nothing you could do that would please God more, and nothing that will ultimately be more fulfilling to you than to carry out the work of having an excellent relationship with God. Read also these words of encouragement from Paul:

> **Colossians 3:1-17 (NLT)** ^{1}Since you have been raised to new life with Christ, set your sights on the realities of heaven, where Christ sits in the place of honor at God's right hand. ^{2}Think about the things of heaven, not the things of earth… ^{5}So put to death the sinful, earthly things lurking within you. Have nothing to do with sexual immorality, impurity, lust, and evil desires. Don't be greedy, for a greedy person is an idolater, worshiping the things of this world…^{8}But now is the time to get rid of anger, rage, malicious behavior, slander, and dirty language… ^{10}Put on your new nature and be renewed as you learn to know your Creator and become like him. ^{12}Since God chose you to be the holy people he loves, you must clothe yourselves with tenderhearted mercy, kindness, humility, gentleness, and patience…^{14}Above all, clothe yourselves with love, which binds us all together in perfect harmony. ^{15}And let the peace that comes from Christ rule in your hearts. For as members of one body you are called to live in peace. And always be thankful. ^{16}Let the message about Christ, in all its

richness, fill your lives. Teach and counsel each other with all the wisdom he gives. Sing psalms and hymns and spiritual songs to God with thankful hearts. [17]And whatever you do or say, do it as a representative of the Lord Jesus, giving thanks through him to God the Father.

Paul is setting out in this passage what the life of a person living in a spiritual palace relationship with God looks like.

In my fourth church appointment, at St. Andrew's United Methodist Church in Brandon Florida, I was the staff representative to the building committee during two huge building construction projects and two building renovation projects. We had a very experienced building committee and chairman, but I was an on-site person for these projects because my office was literally at the construction sites. So I inspected the work multiple times a day, and in the process of all of this I got a firsthand education on the construction of huge buildings (one of the pastoral responsibilities that fall under the category of, "all other responsibilities as may from time to time arise"). One of my happiest memories at that church was that in recognition of my work with the building committee they asked me to drive a front-end loader to ceremonially break ground at the groundbreaking ceremony for the second building we constructed. It was my first time every operating a front-end loader and I surprised myself by managing to do a reasonable job on my first try.

The thing that surprised me most about the construction process was how long it takes for a foundation to be completed. First the entire property is carefully surveyed, and markers are put down outlining the expected dimensions of the construction site. Then soil test drill holes are drilled in the building area to make sure there are no hidden surprises that would threaten the project. Then bulldozers other large machines go to work scraping, leveling, building up and compacting the soil. Then the surveyors came back and the building area is carefully measured for height and levelness and the exact dimensions of the building are measured and staked out and a wooden frame that will hold in the poured concrete is placed. Then about a week of digging and placing the rebar followed; and then the water and sewage pipes and the electrical conduit pipes are placed on top of the rebar and zip tied into place. Then it is concrete day; an entire 18,000 square foot slab would be poured in a day. Truck after truck comes and deposits their cement while workers smoothed it and push it around to fill evenly the entire frame. Then after all is poured and smoothed the entire slab is covered with plastic sheeting and it is allowed to dry for a few days. Then the concrete is smoothed and polished by circular grinders. It takes about four weeks for all that to be done before the construction could begin.

I later found out that a foundation normally takes at about twenty percent of the time of the construction. And you will find that it is pretty much true for constructing a spiritual palace – a lot of time and energy needs to go into preparing the ground and "pouring the concrete" to create your spiritual foundation. If the surveyors improperly measure the location and dimensions of a building all sorts of problems would arise water and sewage pipes wouldn't line up or connect, walls would not match the foundation. In the same way we must know where our heart is, where our mind is, and where our determination level is. Building a spiritual palace relationship with God is more than just adding new ways of thinking (which is already a big accomplishment) and new behaviors; it is also about stopping or changing some negative things we are currently thinking and doing. We have to have our heart right with God, and we have to have the right attitude, or our construction will go wrong, these are the key elements to a spiritual foundation; and that is what this chapter is really about – preparing the ground for our spiritual foundation by doing a self-survey and grinding down our rough spots (taking away the spiritual obstacles in your heart and attitude) that will block our path or skew our construction.

Just as no one would begin constructing a house without knowing exactly where it is to go, we have to know where our heart and mind are. Paul writes the same thing, "Be honest in your evaluation of yourselves, measuring yourselves by the faith God has given us" (Romans 12:3). And, from his second letter to the Corinthians (13:5) "Examine yourselves to see if your faith is genuine. Test yourselves…if not, you have failed the test of genuine faith." Our foundation will only be as strong as we are honest with ourselves about where we are morally and spiritually. Certainly, we must also use the right materials, or our foundation will be weak and shaky at best.

In an earthly construction project, the careful pre-construction survey of the construction site, determines how the ground is to be prepared – it must be built up in some places and flattened out in others. The first part of getting our heart right with God is to survey ourselves, to carefully look at the morality of our behavior and actions. That seems like common sense but when was the last time you did an honest and thorough moral inventory or examination of your conscience? Most people have either never done one or else it has been a very long time and they are in serious need of a repeat.

In Proverbs 30:7-9 we read:

> "O God, I beg two favors from you; let me have them before I die. First, help me never to tell a lie. Second, give me neither poverty nor riches! Give me just enough to satisfy my needs. For if I grow rich, I may deny you and say, "Who is the LORD?" And if I am too poor, I may steal and thus insult God's holy name. (NLT)

This passage points to a significant reality of the human condition: that the business, concerns, and distractions of life can easily cause us to misunderstand or not pay attention to the reality of where we are morally, in terms of our thoughts, words and actions compared to where we would ideally like to be in our relationship with God. We sometimes have a faulty image of our own level of integrity, and many people exaggerate or depreciate their self-value and importance. For us preparing the ground means we cannot go into this effort in denial or lying to ourselves, we must take the time to really look at what we are doing and what we are thinking and what we value.

Jesus said in his Sermon on the Mount that we should not try to take the spec out of our brother's eye when we have a log in our own eye (Matt. 7:3-5). First, he said, we should remove the log from our own eye, then we will be able to see clearly the spec in our brother's eye. His direct lesson was that we shouldn't judge others, but His implied message is twofold: first that we are likely to have blind spots when it comes to ourselves; the log in our eye is our faults that we are ignoring as we look at others. Secondly, the implication is that we should therefore remove our "logs." In other words we should remove or stop doing the faults we have that are displeasing to God. We only can see to remove the logs in our own eyes through self-reflection and self-examination.

Paul's admonitions to evaluate ourselves and test ourselves and Jesus words about removing our log, are just three examples of more than twenty places in the scriptures where we are warned that we need to examine our motives and morals to truly understand where we really are in our relationship with God so we can know where we are going. And several times we are warned if we fail to examine our thoughts and motives and we fail to work to remove our faults, we risk bringing God's judgment upon ourselves. This is another way the Bible is telling us that if we want to move from - just being acceptable to God, to being pleasing God, it starts with our commitment to God to seek excellence in our relationship with Him, and the very next step is to do an honest self-evaluation so we have a clear understanding of what things we must change to reach our goal.

If you are not familiar with the twelve-step program of Alcoholics Anonymous (AA), step 4 of the program calls for a "fearless moral inventory" or what the church has called an "examination of conscience" and this is exactly what we need to do in order to progress. The process AA recommends in carrying out a moral inventory is that you write out your whole life story, to explain all of the bad decisions and mistakes you have made that have gotten to the place you are now. In writing your life story the explanations you give about the decisions you made at crossroad moments reveal the weaknesses in your thought processes. Your other weaknesses and trigger mechanisms are also revealed so that you can see what things you need to overcome to be healthy, and / or succeed in your sobriety. I have seen several of these AA life stories from people I know who are in the program, and they can run to a dozen pages or more. We could all probably benefit from doing that kind of deep moral inventory but at a minimum a moral inventory form such as the one at the end of this chapter can help us know where we are now in terms of our personal integrity and self-valuation.

It is important for all Christians to know what our thought processes are; to realize the weaknesses in our thought processes, and our behavioral weaknesses and trigger mechanisms because everyone who sins has trigger mechanisms and weaknesses and faulty thinking that can lead them to sin. In Proverbs we read, "As a man thinks in his heart so he is" (23:7 KJV). And Paul in his letter to the Romans (12:2) writes, "let God transform you into a new person by changing the way you think... Then you will learn to know God's will for you, which is good and pleasing and perfect." So the scriptures tell that our thought processes are of vital importance to determining our actions. We "let God transform us by changing the way we think" by continually inviting the presence of the Holy Spirit to be inside us, and by continual self-evaluation, and actions to correct any faults that are detected.

When I got out of the Marine Corps, I decided to take a step forward in my spiritual development. I had developed the unfortunate habit of using the Lord's name in vain while in the Corps. I knew that it was breaking the third commandment and I resolved to stop. But for months I struggled without success. One day I was reading something Paul wrote in his first letter to the **(Corinthians 9:27 NLT)** "I discipline my body like an athlete, training it to do what it should. Otherwise, I fear that after preaching to others I myself might be disqualified." It occurred to me that I had not yet tried disciplining my body. So I decided that I would keep track of my words and at the end of the day when I was alone, I would slap myself in the face once for every time I used the Lord's name in vain. Within three days I had stopped completely!

The process of building a spiritual palace relationship with God is a positive upward reinforcing cycle, in which our work and efforts to prepare the ground (our hearts) for God to act and work in our lives through inviting the Holy Spirit, at the same time brings about a transformation of our thoughts and our actions; and the result of the transformation of our thoughts and our actions is an increase in our desire to work to be pleasing to God which improves our relationship with God, causing us to open our heart more to God, which then causes us to invite the Holy Spirit which, starts the process again, leading us in a slow upward spiral towards godliness.

The key to opening our heart to God is daily prayer. At minimum we should pray the Lord's Prayer daily, and if we want to be successful in truly building a spiritual palace we must be constantly (daily) inviting the Holy Spirit to live inside us, to unite with our spirit, and to fill us with the fruit of the Spirit – love, joy, peace, strength, faith, gentleness and kindness, and so to help us with the process of transformation. The good news for us is that Jesus tells us that God is willing to give us the Holy Spirit, "So if you sinful people know how to give good gifts to your children, how much more will your heavenly Father give the Holy Spirit to those who ask him" (Luke 11:13 NLT).

There is no bad news here: God sees us both as we are at this moment, and as we could be. Because of His love and grace God loves us now even while we are yet sinners; he accepts us as we really are, with all of our faults and our failings and our sins, even as He also has a vision of what we can be. Paul tells us: "God showed his great love for us by sending Christ to die for us while we were still sinners" (Romans 5:8). God didn't send us Jesus because we were good, God sent us Jesus because we could not get to good without him – we needed him then and we still all need a savior now. Thankfully, because all of us sin and fall short of the glory of God he sent us Jesus Christ. The apostle John tells us, "God so loved the world so much that he gave His one and only Son, so that everyone who believes in him will not perish but have eternal life" (3:16 NLT). However, even though God does all of this forgiving and accepting of us through Jesus, he is not finished with us, he is calling us to and helping us through the Holy Spirit to grow beyond our old ways and thoughts.

I took this slight detour from the subject of preparing your heart to remind you of God's love for you - just as you are now, because when you examine your conscience, your motives and your morality, using the tools I provide you below, you might be tempted to dislike yourself or to be discouraged. When you examine your conscience, if you at the same time keep in mind God's great love for you - that He sent Christ to die for you to pay for your sins, then your examination of conscience will be an opportunity for thankfulness to God and even joy, and thus, spiritual growth. I know that when my examination reveals all that God forgives me for, because He loves me, I feel thankful and joyful. So remember – since you know that God loves you, if you don't also love yourself you are calling God's judgment into question, since God forgives you, you must also forgive yourself just as you forgive others.

Since examining our conscience is so important to building a spiritual palace I assembled (below) two different examinations of conscience that are easy to use. Either one can be gone through in under thirty minutes, and if you truly reflect on the questions, they raise it will help you prepare the ground in your heart and mind for the foundation of your spiritual palace. They are also good for use on a spiritual retreat and as an annual spiritual tune up or check up to help you evaluate your progress and discern areas where improvement is needed. To use either of these tools effectively you need to set aside some time, at least 20 minutes and preferably an hour, when and where you can be alone and not disturbed. Turn off your phone and take the time to look at your thoughts and behaviors and ask yourself if you are being the person that God created you to be. In these examinations of conscience we are basically asking, "How am I doing in obeying the commandments to love God, to love others, and to love myself?" and, "What in my life is standing in the way of these loves?"

When you look at your actions and thoughts and values some things will be quickly obvious. For instance, I don't need to examine my conscience to know that I have an anger problem when I am driving. I don't have to look very deeply into myself to know that I am not patient enough. But I benefit from examining my conscience to see what I am doing about it and what I could be doing. Quite often the work you need to do, the changes you need to make are not as obvious to you as they may be to those around you. Denial (da Nile), as they say, is not just a river in Egypt; in reality all of us have blind spots when it comes to looking at ourselves. All of us have as Jesus mentioned logs in our own eyes. Like me, you also are probably multilayered: some of your faults and negative traits are on or close to the surface, but the causes of them and the level of commitment you are making in response to them may be hidden from your sight.

Maybe on a deeper level, not so obvious to the world, you have some bad trait you would be at least a bit embarrassed if lots of people knew about: it could be insecurity, doubt, pride, lust, anger, laziness, etc. We know on some level what our sins are, but we tend to hide them from others and to justify them to ourselves instead of just confronting them and eliminating them. Unfortunately, sometimes the negative traits that afflict us are buried deep in our subconscious minds. they can be the result of things that happened a long time ago in your life, and for one reason or another you don't realize how they are still affecting you today. People who received abuse as a child, either physical or verbal, or whose family life was a string of broken or troubled relationships, often internalize a poor self-image without realizing it.

My own experience as a young teenager is that my Dad was an alcoholic and I internalized thought patterns and behaviors resulting from without even realizing what they were and how they were affecting my behavior. In fact I didn't even face the reality that my dad was an alcoholic until I was seventeen even though it should have been quite obvious. It wasn't until I was in counseling in my thirties that I processed and was able to move past the abuse I received. That is how denial works. The messages I received and internalized diminished my self-esteem and confidence. I self-medicated with alcohol and pot to try and build my self-esteem; and I was partially successful in building my confidence through joining the Marines and picking up lots of young women as a bouncer in a disco. I am not trying to excuse bad behavior I am just trying to point out that preparing the ground for the foundation of your spiritual palace can be a long and difficult process. It may require many professional counseling sessions to fully restructure your thinking in order to proceed in constructing your spiritual palace.

In this chapter we have heard that building a spiritual palace relationship with God starts with preparing the ground by looking deeply and honestly at our self, measuring our conscience, our morality and motives, with honesty and identifying those areas where we know we have work to be done. So I want to ask you to take twenty minutes to an hour this week to follow the instructions for one of the examinations of conscience below so you can get started on, or make further progress in, constructing your spiritual palace. Will you do that?

Please join me in a prayer:

> Lord God, Paul wrote that we must no longer be children, that we must grow up in every way into him who is the head, into Christ; and that all of us should come to the measure of the full stature of Christ. (Ephesians 4:15). We know that this is part of your invitation to us to receive the best thing this life has to offer – to reach the heights of an excellent relationship with You God. We know Lord that you invite us both for our good, for our own benefit, and also for the benefit of others we are in relationship with. Help us God open our hearts to you daily and invite you Holy Spirit to come and live inside us daily. Help us see what we need to change and have the wisdom to know how to do what we must do to be closer to you. In Jesus name we pray. Amen.

Scripture Quotes
Chapter Five: Preparing the Ground

Ephesians 4:13-16 (NRSV) [13]until <u>all of us come to</u> the unity of the faith and of the knowledge of the Son of God, to <u>maturity, to the measure of the full stature of Christ.</u> [14]We must no longer be children, tossed to and fro and blown about by every wind of doctrine, by people's trickery, by their craftiness in deceitful scheming. [15]But speaking the truth in love, <u>we must grow up in every way into him who is the head, into Christ,</u> [16]from whom the whole body, joined and knit together by every ligament with which it is equipped, as each part is working properly, promotes <u>the body's growth in building itself up</u> in love.

Romans 12:2-3 (NLT) ²Don't copy the behavior and customs of this world, but <u>let God transform you into a new person by changing the way you think</u>. Then you will learn to know God's will for you, which is good and pleasing and perfect. ³Because of the privilege and authority God has given me, I give each of you this warning: <u>Don't think you are better than you really are. Be honest in your evaluation of yourselves, measuring yourselves by the faith God has given us.</u>

2 Corinthians 13:5 (NLT) <u>Examine yourselves to see if your faith is genuine. Test yourselves.</u> Surely you know that Jesus Christ is among you; <u>if not, you have failed the test of genuine faith.</u>

Matthew 7:3-5 (TEV) ³Why, then, do you look at the speck in your brother's eye and <u>pay</u> no <u>attention to the log in your own eye</u>? ⁴How dare you say to your brother, 'Please, let me take that speck out of your eye,' when you have a log in your own eye? ⁵You hypocrite! First <u>take the log out of your own eye, and then you will be able to see clearly to take the speck out of your brother's eye.</u>

Proverbs 23:7 (NKJV) For <u>as he thinks in his heart, so *is* he</u>. "Eat and drink!" he says to you, but his heart is not with you

Luke 11:13 (NLT) ¹³So if you sinful people know how to give good gifts to your children, how much more will your heavenly Father give the Holy Spirit to those who ask him."

Romans 5:8 (NLT) ⁸But <u>God showed his great love for us by sending Christ to die for us while we were still sinners.</u>

Galatians 6:3-4 (TEV) ³<u>If you think you are something when you really are nothing, you are only deceiving yourself.</u> ⁴You should each judge your own conduct. If it is good, then you can be proud of what you yourself have done, without having to compare it with what someone else has done.

1 Corinthians 11:27-29 (NLT) ²⁷So anyone who eats this bread or drinks this cup of the Lord unworthily is guilty of sinning against the body and blood of the Lord. ²⁸That is why you should examine yourself before eating the bread and drinking the cup. ²⁹For if you eat the bread or drink the cup without honoring the body of Christ, you are eating and drinking God's judgment upon yourself.

An Examination of Conscience

I. Start by giving God thanks for the many blessings you have received throughout your lifetime. Mention at least 10 things you are thankful for, including such things as your life, faith, love, etc.

II. Ask God for His help and grace to know what your sins are so that you may be rid of them. Examples of troublesome characteristics and traits (also termed "character defects") that would belong in an inventory are pride, resentment, gluttony, guilt, lust, anger, envy, sloth, fear, etc.

III. Ask God to help you see clearly how you got to this point in your life: what are the assumptions you made, the thoughts behind the bad traits that you have accumulated.

IV. Ask God for His help and grace to know what sins you may have committed this day by thought, word or action (you can use the questions from either or both of the Examinations of Conscience below).

V. After you have completed your examination of conscience ask God for forgiveness for your shortcomings.

VI. Ask God to fill you with his Holy Spirit to help you to do better and to conquer or not repeat this sin (these sins) in the future.

VII. Thank God for His love and grace and forgiveness given to you freely – the example of which is God sending his son to be an offering for our sins, and it is confirmed to us by the action of the Holy Spirit within us.

A Condensed Version of John Wesley's Questions for the Examination of Self

1. Am I honest in all my acts and words, or do I exaggerate?

2. Am I self-conscious, self-pitying, or self-justifying?

3. Did I give the Bible time to speak to me today?

4. Did I pray and give the God time to speak to me today?

5. When did I last speak to someone else about my faith?

6. Do I disobey God in anything?

7. Do I insist upon doing something about which my conscience is uneasy?

8. Am I jealous, impure, critical, irritable, touchy, or distrustful?

9. Is there anyone whom I fear, dislike, disown, criticize, hold resentment toward or disregard? If so, what am I doing about it?

10. Do I grumble or complain constantly?

An Examination of Conscience Based on the 10 Commands of Moses, the 2 Great Commandments of Jesus, And the Qualities of Love described by Paul in 1 Corinthians 13

• "I am the Lord your God…Worship no god but me." TEV Exodus 20:1-17 Have **I loved any person or anything more than God?**

• "Do not bow down to any idol or worship it," **Are any things such as my job, my career, my possessions etc. more important to me than God is?**

- "Do not use my name for evil purposes," **Do I curse using the name of God or Jesus when I am angry? Do I claim to know what God wants in order to get a person or people to do what I want?**

- "Observe the Sabbath day and keep it holy." **Do I go to church every Sunday or at least take a special time to worship God once a week?**

- Honor your father and your mother. (NLT) **Do I respect my parents? Do I show that respect by my actions?**

- "Do not commit murder." (TEV) **Am I currently wishing anyone dead?**

- "Do not commit adultery." **Jesus included looking lustfully in this category.**

- "Do not steal." **Am I honest with work supplies? Expense accounts? My tax returns? All such matters?**

- "Do not accuse anyone falsely." **Have I lied about someone or about something someone said to advance my cause or make myself look better, or to harm that person, or just compulsively?**

- "You must not covet your neighbor's house...your neighbor's wife, or anything else that belongs to your neighbor." **Am I satisfied with the things I have or am I always wanting more? Do I daydream and wish I had more money or things?**

The 2 Great Commandments of Jesus

• Do I love the Lord with all of my heart, mind, soul and strength?

• Do I love my neighbor as I love myself?

• Do I love myself as Christ loves me?

And the Qualities of Love described by Paul in 1 Corinthians 13

• Love is patient… am I?

• Love is kind… am I?

• Love is not jealous… am I?

• Love is not boastful or proud or rude… am I?

• Love does not demand its own way… do I?

• Love is not easily angered… Am I?

• Love forgives easily… do I?

• Love rejoices whenever truth and justice win out… do I?

• Love never gives up, or loses faith, but is always hopeful, and endures through every circumstance…

• Do I?

Return to **V** above.

Chapter Six: Money is an Obstacle or a Tool

Originally preached October 13, 2019

When I was serving a church in Gouldsboro Pennsylvania the church added a new fellowship hall. One of the contractors and the church got into a dispute about the amount of the final payment because when the contractor was preparing the ground to place the foundation for the new building, he discovered that the little stone sticking up in the construction site was actually the tip of an 80-ton boulder! It took all kinds of specialized machinery to get that stone removed, and the contractor had not figured that into his charges. In this chapter I want to talk about what could look like a little stumbling block in your spiritual life, but what could be an 80-ton boulder blocking your spiritual progress: your giving to God?

Would you join me in prayer?

Lord God, you know us better than we know ourselves. You know what is good for us and You always want what is best for us. You desire that we remove the obstacles and barriers that keep us from full participation in Your plans for us. These barriers once we remove them open us up to Your blessings and to spiritual growth, so help us we pray Father to see what barriers we need to remove; help us to have the wisdom and determination to do so. Thank You Lord.

When I finished this book and sent it in to the publisher, I got back the galleys to fix any typos, and I was still working on that when I had to write the sermon this chapter was based on. As I began writing the sermon I prayed, "God this is Your sermon, Your message for Your people; what would You like to say to Your people about stewardship?" God quickly and powerfully answered my prayer. His answer: *God is very serious about our giving. God wants us to know that our giving is one of the most important things that we do as Christians; God knows what we give and the amount we give is important to God.* After the worship services were over and I was sitting at home on Sunday afternoon, I realized that the message God gave me needed to be added to this book.

To be quite honest I was surprised, not at the speed or intensity of God's answer, but at the content of God's answer. I have been a pastor for 35 years and I had never before realized or been taught about the depth and intensity of God's feelings about giving. As I researched for the sermon I realized that I had been taken by surprise by God's feelings about giving, because the importance of our giving is something that has been largely lost or diminished in the transition of the Christian people of God, from an Old Testament based religion to a New Testament based religion.

It is widely known that there are 613 laws in the Old Testament, and Christians have largely abandoned almost all of them, seeing them replaced by what Jesus told us: that all the laws are replaced by the two commandments to love God, and to love others as we love ourselves. Christians have completely abandoned the Jewish Old Testament system of animal sacrifices, seeing the sacrifice of Jesus dying on the cross as replacing or eliminating any need for further sacrifice (Hebrews 10:1-18). However, while the death of Christ took away the need for animal sacrifice, it did not take away our need to give offerings or change how important it is to God that we give appropriately to God.

In order to get a fuller understanding of the importance of our offerings to God it is important to look at how important offerings are in the Old Testament. One giant clue for us is the fact that the word *offering*, or *offerings* is mentioned more times in the Old Testament (a total of 848 times) than the words worship, praise, & love combined (a total of 832 times). In fact,

848 mentions is almost an average of once on every page in the Old Testament. That alone should let you know how important offerings are in the Old Testament. Those of us who are familiar with the Pentateuch (first five books of the Bible) know that large sections of Exodus, Leviticus, Numbers and Deuteronomy are spent telling in great detail what the different kinds of offerings and sacrifices are, who should handle them, how they should be handled, what should be done with them afterwards, and what makes them unacceptable to God.

In the Old Testament, sacrifices and offerings were how the people got their sins forgiven. The giving of a sacrifice is not giving God a bribe; a sacrifice is something that costs you dearly, so you give it because you are sorry for, and want forgiveness for your sin that required the sacrifice, and sorry for the loss it costs you. In those days, if your offering was not accepted by God, that was terrible news, because it meant not only were you not forgiven, you were therefore likely to be punished or at least corrected by God. The story of Cain and Able (found in Genesis 4) is an example.

When it was time for the harvest, Cain and Abel decide to give a thank offering to God. Abel brought the best of his new lambs from his flock. Cain brought some of whatever he harvested. God accepted Abel's offering because it represented his best, and he rejected Cain's offering because it was not his best, it did not reflect faith or a sacrifice. Cain was so dejected and angry and jealous that he killed his brother.

Cain was trying to give the minimum to God, but Abel was giving from the heart and giving his best. We could say that Cain was trying to appease God, but Abel was trying to please God. The Lord didn't punish Cain for his unacceptable offering; instead he warned Cain about his offerings, and that warning is still valid for us today. God tells Cain about his offerings: "If you do what is right you will be accepted, but if you don't, then sin is crouching at your door, waiting to take over your life."

The message to us is: if we don't do what is right by God with our offerings, we too are opening a door for sin to come in our lives.

Another example of the important of giving an acceptable offering to God is found in Malachi. The Lord Almighty says,

"Children honor their parents, and servants honor their masters. I am your father—why don't you honor me? I am your master—why don't you respect me? You despise me, and yet you ask, 'How have we despised you?' 7This is how—by offering worthless food on my altar. Then you ask, 'How have we failed to respect you?' I will tell you—by showing contempt for my altar. 8 When you bring a blind or sick or lame animal to sacrifice to me, do you think there's nothing wrong with that? Try giving an animal like that to the governor! Would he be pleased with you or grant you any favors?" Now, you priests, try asking God to be good to us. He will not answer your prayer, and it will be your fault.

So we see here, as we saw with Cain, that the anger of God is turned towards those who claim to believe in him and yet offer less than they should.

Beginning about 750 BC the Old Testament prophets brought a number of messages from God to correct the thoughts and actions of the people of God. The message of the prophets about offerings was given to correct a mistaken idea that many people apparently had about offerings - that they were automatically forgiven just because they made an offering or sacrifice. The prophets were letting us know that our offerings are judged by God based not as much on what we give, but on what is in our heart and how our actions reflect what is in our heart. In Amos (5:21-24 NRSV) we read Amos quoting God saying:

"I hate, I despise your festivals, and I take no delight in your solemn assemblies. Even though you offer me your burnt offerings and grain offerings, I will not accept them; and the offerings of well-being of your fatted animals I will not look upon. Take away from me the noise of your songs; I will not listen to the melody of your harps. But let justice roll down like waters, and righteousness like an ever-flowing stream."

The message here is that justice and righteousness are more important to God than material offerings. We see the same message in a different format in the book of the prophet Micah

"With what shall I come before the LORD, and bow myself before God on high? Shall I come before him with burnt offerings, with calves a year old? Will the LORD be pleased with thousands of rams, with ten thousands of rivers of oil? Shall I give my firstborn for my transgression, the fruit of my body for the sin of my soul?" He has told you, O mortal, what is good; and what does the LORD require of you but to do justice, and to love kindness, and to walk humbly with your God? (Micah 6:6-8 NRSV)

This is a slightly different take on it in Micah, but to God, justice, kindness, and being humble are more important than tons of money.

In the Old Testament (OT) animals, grain, bread, olive oil and money were all used as offerings. A key difference between the Old and New Testaments is that in the OT the priests were the key: all offerings and scarifies has to be given to the Priests who would then offer them on behalf of the giver (Leviticus 2:8 & 5:8). It was against the law for a person to sacrifice an animal to God on their own (Leviticus 17:8-9). The Pentateuch requires that priests can only be from the tribe of the Levites. They had to be specially consecrated and dressed in priestly attire (Exodus 28), and they had to perform the rituals for the different types of sacrifices, in the way that was carefully described in the Bible.

There are a half dozen different types of offerings described in the Old Testament, and the priests had to make them all. There was a *sin offering* – made to take away the guilt of your sin (that required the sacrifice or death of an animal). There is a *thank offering* just to say thank you God for my blessings, and a *votive offering* which is saying thanks for a specific thing that you vowed to God or prayed for and that God did. There are *offerings for specific projects*, building and maintenance; there is *a tribute offering* – or *first fruits offering*, and there is a *freewill offering* given just to honor God. With all these offerings the individual brought the offering to the priests and the priest made the offering to God on their behalf.

Now all of this is the old system; it starts to fail when the temple in Jerusalem is destroyed by the Babylonians in 586 BC. The temple was rebuilt by Ezra and Zerubbabel in 430 BC, and animal sacrifice resumed, but it ended completely and permanently when the Romans destroyed the temple in 70 A.D., as a part of the First Jewish Roman war. By the time the New Testament was being written the whole old system of Priests receiving and making offerings of animals, and food and oil was gone, and Christians were no longer worshipping at synagogues but independently.

What Christianity has retained here from its Jewish heritage is the regular offering of money and a modified version of the tithe. Jesus said we should tithe (Matthew 23:23). And the churches have taken guidance on giving from the Apostle Paul's simple commandment (1 Corinthians 16:1-2):

"Now regarding your question about the money being collected for God's people in Jerusalem. You should follow the same procedure I gave to the churches in Galatia. On the first day of each week, you should each put aside a portion of the money you have earned."

The New Testament system is so much simpler than the old system; as a pastor I am really glad that clergy no longer need to sacrifice animals! But what gets lost in the transition from the elaborate Old Testament system of offerings and sacrifices, to the simplicity of the New Testament weekly offering, and what I heard from God when I prayed about this, is the very real anger of God that is directed towards those who say they belong to Him but fail to honor God by giving God what they should.

Jesus and Paul were preaching mostly to convert Jews to Christianity. These were Jews who were brought up with the Old Testament system, and who better understood how important making a proper offering to God is. But in our focus on our sins being forgiven through the sacrifice of Jesus, we modern Christians have lost our focus on how important it is to God that we give appropriate offerings. Honoring God with our offerings is an essential key to our spiritual healthiness: giving appropriately opens our hearts and our lives to receive great blessings from God. Failing to honor God properly with our offerings is an obstacle to God's grace in our lives; it is the 80-ton boulder that prevents a solid spiritual foundation from being poured.

You cannot successfully build a spiritual palace relationship with God if you are holding back any part of yourself: who you are, what you do and what you have, and that includes our money. Withholding anything that we should give to God, whether it is prayer time, or service, or our money, leads to spiritual unhealthiness, as it did with Cain. Jesus told us, "Store up for yourselves treasures in heaven, where neither moth nor rust consumes and where thieves do not break in and steal. For where your treasure is, there your heart will be also" (Matthew 6:20-21 NRSV). Failing to honor God properly with our offerings means our hearts are not in the right place; that means our hearts are closed to God and to God's blessings, and it also means we are subject to God's anger and discipline.

A pastor friend of mine likes to say, "you cannot out give God." What he means is God gives back to us monetarily and spiritually in proportion to what we give. Here is what Jesus said:

"Give to others, and God will give to you. Indeed, you will receive a full measure, a generous helping, poured into your hands—all that you can hold. The measure you use for others is the one that God will use for you" (Luke 6:38 TEV).

Paul also said virtually the same thing in his second letter to the Corinthians.

Remember this—a farmer who plants only a few seeds will get a small crop. But the one who plants generously will get a generous crop... For God is the one who provides seed for the farmer and then bread to eat. In the same way, he will provide and increase your resources and then produce a great harvest of generosity in you. Yes, you will be enriched in every way so that you can always be generous (2 Corinthians 9:6, 10-11 NLT).

So, the Bible, my experience and the experience of the members of every congregation I have served, is that when we are generous to God, God is generous to us in return. Paul is saying that when we are generous in giving because of our desire to please God, God blesses us with more than we need so that we can continue to be generous.

There are two simple keys to honoring God properly with your offerings. The first is to give in proportion to what you have. Jesus was at the temple one day watching people come and giving their offerings for the temple, that is for the maintenance of the temple. He saw a poor woman come and give two small copper coins and Jesus said that she gave more than anyone else, because she gave all she had to live on. The message from that for us is that someone like Bill Gates can give $10 billion dollars and you can give $10 dollars and you still gave more in the eyes of God that Bill Gates did. It is what the offering means to you and that it is from your heart that is important to God. So, the first key is: give in proportion to what you have.

The second of the simple keys to honoring God properly with your offerings is to be generous towards God. Cain was trying to appease God, and his offering was rejected. Abel was trying to please God and his offering was accepted. It seems the Biblical message is that when it comes to offerings there is no appeasing God; there is either pleasing God or not pleasing God. God is patient with us, and if we are starting out in the giving business, we can start in our giving to God with giving enough to appease God so that God is not angry with us, as long as we are intentional about moving towards becoming pleasing to God.

When I became a pastor, I was poor: minimum salary for a pastor in upstate New York qualified my family for government food assistance, and I gave what I thought I could afford. But in time I served larger churches, I was not poor anymore so I could give more. But more importantly, I realized I needed to lead by example: that as a spiritual leader I needed to be able to ask others to do as I am doing, not just as I say. I also had a strong desire, as a person who loves Jesus, to do more than just appease God, I wanted to please God, so my wife Anna and I made the decision to move our giving level to and beyond the Biblical tithe.

I still use the Biblical tithe as my model. Tithe is an old English word that means one tenth. A tithe is 10% of your harvest (I always say today it would be a tenth of your after-tax income for the year). According to the Bible (Deuteronomy 14:22-28), tithes are given every year, but in a three-year cycle. In two of the three years, the Bible says to use the tithe to honor God and your relationship with God with your family, by giving gifts, enjoying great food, and celebrating. In the third year you are to give your whole tithe to the church (in those days – the leaders of your synagogue, the Levites in your town), and the church uses your tithe to help it feed the poor and provide for the upkeep of the church.

If we are going to follow Paul's advice and set aside a portion of our income every week for an offering, and if we are going to follow the Biblical tithe model, then based on Deuteronomy 14 with its three year cycle, that means we take the third year tithe (which we are to give entirely to God) and divide it up by three years which comes to an average of 3.3% per year. A lot of preachers like to ignore the part of Deuteronomy 14 that says we should take our tithe in two of the three years of the cycle and, "Spend it on whatever you want—beef, lamb, wine, beer—and there, in the presence of the Lord your God, you and your families are to eat and enjoy yourselves." They want to claim we should give a tenth to the church every year, and if we don't then God will be angry, but that is clearly not what the Bible says.

So, two related points: first that we need to make sure we are taking 3.3% of our income every year to give to God through the church or some other charity (but preferably church). And second, we also need to set aside 6.6% of our income every year to honor God with by giving gifts to, and celebrating God with our family members, because God wants us to celebrate, to appreciate the material blessings God has given us as a part of our faith life. Lastly, if we want to grow spiritually it is important that we are generous in our giving to God. Deuteronomy also tells us:

"Give freely and spontaneously. Don't have a stingy heart. The way you handle matters like this triggers God, your God's, blessing in everything you do, all your work and ventures" (Deuteronomy 15:10 TM).

So, in addition to our tithe, it is important to be generous towards God and others.

Increasing your giving to God is one of the most concrete steps you can take to building up your spiritual palace relationship with God. I like to point out that giving to God is the only place in the whole Bible where God challenges us to put Him to the test:

"Bring the full tithe into the storehouse, so that there may be food in my house, and thus put me to the test, says the LORD of hosts; see if I will not open the windows of heaven for you and pour down for you an overflowing blessing" (Malachi 3:10 NRSV).

I know that giving to God what you should will bless you, and if you are not already doing so I challenge you to test God by your giving. I know you will be blessed.

Will you join me in prayer?

Lord God, You want us to give not because You need what we give but because we need to give for the good of our own soul and for the sake of our spiritual growth. Help us Lord to trust in You, to reach into our purse or wallet or accounts and give to You what You desire for us, knowing it will make a better happier us. Thank You Lord!

Questions for reflection and discussion.

Are you giving to appease God or to please God?
Are you giving in proportion to your income?
Are you being generous towards God?
Why are you giving what you give?
Are you going to do anything differently now? Why or why not?

Scripture Quotes & Sermon Notes
Stewardship Is a Way of Life

Genesis 4:3-8 (NLT) When it was time for the harvest, Cain presented some of his crops as a gift to the LORD. 4Abel also brought a gift—the best of the firstborn lambs from his flock. The LORD accepted Abel and his gift, but he did not accept Cain and his gift. This made Cain very angry, and he looked dejected. 6"Why are you so angry?" the LORD asked Cain. "Why do you look so dejected? 7You will be accepted if you do what is right. But if you refuse to do what is right, then watch out! Sin is crouching at the door, eager to control you. But you must subdue it and be its master." 8One day Cain suggested to his brother, "Let's go out into the fields." And while they were in the field, Cain attacked his brother, Abel, and killed him.

Malachi 1:6-14 (TEV) 6The Lord Almighty says to the priests, "Children honor their parents, and servants honor their masters. I am your father—why don't you honor me? I am your master—<u>why don't you respect me? You despise me,</u> and yet you ask, 'How have we despised you?' 7This is how—by offering worthless food on my altar. Then you ask, 'How have we failed to respect you?' I will tell you—by showing contempt for my altar. 8 When you bring a blind or sick or lame animal to sacrifice to me, do you think there's nothing wrong with that? Try giving an animal like that to the governor! Would he be pleased with you or grant you any favors?" 9Now, you priests, try asking <u>God</u> to be good to us. He <u>will not answer your prayer, and it will be your fault</u>.

Amos 5:21-24 (NRSV) I hate, I despise your festivals, and I take no delight in your solemn assemblies. Even though you offer me your burnt offerings and grain offerings, I will not accept them; and the offerings of well-being of your fatted animals I will not look upon… I will not listen to the melody of your harps. But <u>let justice roll down like waters, and righteousness like an ever-flowing stream</u>.

Micah 6:6-8 "With what shall I come before the LORD, and bow myself before God on high? Shall I come before him with burnt offerings, with calves a year old? Will the LORD be pleased with thousands of rams, with ten thousand of rivers of oil? Shall I give my firstborn for my transgression, the fruit of my body for the sin of my soul?" He has told you, O mortal, what is good; and <u>what does the LORD require of you but to do justice, and to love kindness, and to walk humbly with your God</u>?

Matthew 23:23 (NLT) "What sorrow awaits you teachers of religious law and you Pharisees. Hypocrites! For you are careful to tithe even the tiniest income from your herb gardens, but you ignore the more important aspects of the law—justice, mercy, and faith. <u>You should tithe, yes</u>, but do not neglect the more important things.

Mark 12:41-44 (NIV) Jesus sat down opposite the place where the offerings were put and watched the crowd putting their money into the temple treasury. Many rich people threw in large amounts. ⁴²But a poor widow came and put in two very small copper coins. Calling his disciples to him, Jesus said, "I tell you the truth, <u>this poor widow has put more into the treasury than all the others</u>. ⁴⁴They all gave out of their wealth; but she, out of her poverty, put in everything—all she had to live on."

Malachi 3:10 (NRSV) Bring the full tithe into the storehouse, so that there may be food in my house, and thus put me to the <u>test</u>, says the LORD of hosts; <u>see if I will not open the windows of heaven for you and pour down for you an overflowing blessing</u>.

2 Corinthians 9:6-15 (NLT) Remember this—a farmer who plants only a few seeds will get a small crop. But the one who plants generously will get a generous crop. 7You must each decide in your heart how much to give. And don't give reluctantly or in response to pressure. "For God loves a person who gives cheerfully." 8And God will generously provide all you need. Then you will always have everything you need, and plenty left over to share with others… For God is the one who provides seed for the farmer and then bread to eat. In the same way, he will provide and increase your resources and then produce a great harvest of generosity in you. 11Yes, you will be enriched in every way so that you can always be generous. And when we take your gifts to those who need them, they will thank God. 12So two good things will result from this ministry of giving—the needs of the believers in Jerusalem will be met, and they will joyfully express their thanks to God. 13As a result of your ministry, they will give glory to God. For your generosity to them and to all believers will prove that you are obedient to the Good News of Christ. 14And they will pray for you with deep affection because of the overflowing grace God has given to you. 15Thank God for this gift too wonderful for words!

Deuteronomy 14:22-29 (TEV) 22 "Set aside a tithe—a tenth of all that your fields produce each year. 23Then go to the one place where the Lord your God has chosen to be worshiped; and there in his presence eat the tithes of your grain, wine, and olive oil, and the first-born of your cattle and sheep. Do this so that you may learn to honor the Lord your God always. 24If the place of worship is too far from your home for you to carry there the tithe of the produce that the Lord has blessed you with, then do this: 25Sell your produce and take the money with you to the one place of worship. 26Spend it on whatever you want—beef, lamb, wine, beer—and there, in the presence of the Lord your God, you and your families are to eat and enjoy yourselves. 27"Do not neglect the Levites who live in your towns; they have no property of their own. 28At the end of every third year bring the tithe of all your crops and store it in your towns. 29This food is for the Levites, since they own no property, and for the foreigners, orphans, and widows who live in your towns. They are to come and get all they need. Do this, and the Lord your God will bless you in everything you do.

Luke 6:38 (NLT) Give, and it will be given to you. A good measure, pressed down, shaken together, running over, will be put into your lap; for the measure you give will be the measure you get back.

Deuteronomy 15:10 (TM) Give freely and spontaneously. Don't have a stingy heart. The way you handle matters like this triggers God, your God's, blessing in everything you do, all your work and ventures. 11There are always going to be poor and needy people among you. So I command you: Always be generous, open purse and hands, give to your neighbors in trouble, your poor and hurting neighbors.

Chapter Seven: The Foundation
The Six Ingredients of a Spiritual A Foundation

Originally preached February 24, 2019

In Chapter Five we prepared the ground for our foundation through doing an examination of conscience. In this chapter I will talk about the six basic elements required to pour a solid foundation that we can build a spiritual palace relationship with God upon. Regular concrete is made of 6 elements: calcium, silicon, aluminum, iron, water, and sand/gravel; without any of these six ingredients you don't have strong concrete. Doing an examination of conscience or a moral inventory is the first of the six ingredients – and it helps us make progress towards the other ingredients of a successful foundation to build an excellent relationship with God. In addition to self-examination, the other ingredients are humility, desire to know God, desire to be pleasing to God, love, (that is loving God, neighbor and self), and we ourselves are the sand and gravel of the mix. But before I get too far into the substance of all that I want to start with a funny story that is related to the message:

A young construction worker was bragging to the other guys at the construction site about how strong he is. And he was particularly getting after a couple of the older guys and making fun of them and saying I am so much stronger than you are, and so on and so on. One of the older guys said, "Well why don't you put your money where your mouth is," he said. "I'll bet you $20 dollars that I can wheel something across this site in this wheelbarrow that you won't be able to wheel back." The guy says, "You're on!"

The old guy picks up the wheelbarrow, and he says "Okay, Get in."

Would you join me in prayer?

> Gracious Lord I thank you for the privilege and responsibility of doing the work of building a spiritual palace. May all that is written and read here be acceptable in your sight, and may it serve to lift me closer to You for You are my creator, my redeemer and my sustainer.

A moral inventory or an examination of conscience is the first ingredient of the concrete of our foundation because the first result of a moral inventory done properly, is the second ingredient in our spiritual concrete - humility. Humility is foundational, an essential element to a solid spiritual foundation. A lack of humility is an obstacle to God; if we are not humble, we will block out God's ability to work inside us with the Holy Spirit. Just like concrete that is lacking calcium will not allow the other elements to bond properly, humility is vital to allow the rest of our spiritual foundation to form strong and solid. The prophet Isaiah wrote: "God dwells with those who are contrite and humble in spirit" (57:14-15). Humility helps us see more clearly the logs in our eyes that we cannot see if we are not humble and that we need to remove if we want to be pleasing to God.

In some of the Methodist Disciple Bible study curriculum there is a weekly segment called The Radical Disciple. Their brand of radical is really not radical, unless you think that taking our discipleship seriously is radical. I think *Radical Methodists* is an oxymoron, but Jesus practiced truly radical humility. His humility was so far over the top, so far in excess of what we might consider to be normal that it is just amazing. I will give you a few examples. A religious leader, a teacher of the religious laws came up to Jesus and asked him this question: "Good Teacher, what should I do to inherit eternal life?" Jesus replied with amazing humility; he said to him, "Why do you call me good?" Jesus added. "Only God is truly good." So Jesus is putting himself in second place to God acknowledging his place in his relationship God.

Jesus taught his disciples humility repeatedly and gave them examples in his actions that we should be humble. He taught that we should see children as our models for the attitude we should have if we want to enter heaven. We should not judge others, and we should not look down on others because of their sins, recognizing that we also are sinners. And he also taught, "those of you who want to be great must be servants and whoever wants to be the greatest of you all must be a servant of all. For even the Son of man (talking about himself) came not to be served but to serve others and to give his life as a sacrifice or a ransom for many." Now when we think about the spiritual power that Jesus had at his command, to be able to heal the sick, to raise the dead, to be able to walk on water, to feed 5000 people with a few loaves of bread and a few fish, and yet, he said he was the servant of all.

And he demonstrated this radical humility with his actions - in washing his disciple's feet at the last Supper. Now the part of the whole story of Jesus washing the disciples' feet that really blows my mind is not just that he would wash their feet, but that he washed Judas' feet. Jesus knew that Judas was about to leave and go betray him, and that the result of that betrayal was going to be his arrest. He knew that he was going to be subjected to a horrible whipping with a lead tipped roman whip, and that he was going to be put to death in the most horrible way imaginable, a crucifixion. Knowing all that Jesus washed Judas' feet! Now that is not just an act of forgiveness it is an act of amazing humility because he is being humble before God. He is saying to God in that act, "Whatever you have in store for me, whatever path you have laid out for me I am willing to walk." And that is the most amazing level of humility.

One of my favorite theologians is Thomas Merton. Thomas Merton was a catholic priest and a brilliant theologian. And he wrote this: "Pride makes us artificial, and <u>humility makes us real</u>." Read that again, "Pride makes us artificial, and <u>humility makes us real</u>." I like that definition because what humility really is, is facing reality, facing the truth of where we are morally and ethically, and the truth for us is that we really do need God. We recognize that God is not just our creator, but really is our redeemer through Jesus Christ. Confronting our sins makes us realize or reminds that we need a redeemer. So humility is about acknowledging that we need God, and there is nothing wrong with that, that is a great thing.

The next three ingredients of our spiritual concrete go together; they are three desires: the desire to know God, the desire to please God, and the desire to love the Lord our God with all of our heart. These three go together because each one, when we strengthen it, it strengthens the others. Brother Lawrence, a 17th century Carmelite monk was widely known as a saintly man, a man who was very close to God. He never wrote a book himself, but he was so impressive in his humility and wisdom that a member of his community followed him around for a couple of months, just picking his brain and writing down his thoughts and philosophies to write a book entitled *The Practice of the Presence of God*. He quoted Brother Lawrence saying this:

> "Let us occupy ourselves entirely in knowing God. The more we know Him, the more we will desire to know Him. As love increases with knowledge, the more we know God, the more we will truly love God…"

And so the desire to know God, the desire to please God, and the desire to love the Lord our God with all of our heart work together. The more we know God the more we love God, the more we love God the more we want to please God. The more we desire to be pleasing to God the more we seek to know God, and so on. This is another example of a positive upward reinforcing cycle in our relationship with God: together each holy desire reinforces the other. The desires to grow in our love of God, in our knowledge of God, and to be pleasing to God are different from an earthly foundation because in a spiritual palace relationship with God they continue to grow throughout our lifetime.

The word *humble* is from the Latin word *humilis* meaning low, as in down to the earth. I mentioned in the beginning of the chapter that we ourselves are like the sand and gravel of the mix. Ironically, the book of Genesis says that Adam was made from the soil or dirt of the earth. In Hebrew the word for earth is *adama*, so Adam is made of adama; to Hebrew speakers Adam is literally earth man, the man made from earth. Our bodies are made up of basically the same elements you find in soil and sea water. Our bodies, our minds, the totality of who we are and all that we have all needs to be put into the mix of our spiritual foundation. Our willingness to give God everything – if asked – is the final ingredient.

If I take a bag of ready-mix concrete and put it into a wheelbarrow it stays in that powdered form, no stronger than a handful of sand until water is added. And as soon as water is added it activates a chemical reaction that transforms the chemistry of the ingredients and turns them into a form of hardened mineral which is concrete. The water for all the ingredients of our spiritual foundation, the activating factor is love – love of God, love of our neighbors and love of ourselves. "God is love" John tells us, if we live in love we live in God and God lives in us (1 John 4:16-17); that is where the activating power comes from. Love in us takes that mixture of ourselves and our self-awareness and our humility and our desire to know God and be pleasing to God it takes all those elements and activates them, empowers them, and makes us true children of God and makes us like that concrete: much stronger than we would be with any of those elements individually. Together they make an amazingly solid rock foundation than can support us in any test that life provides.

God shows His love is to us in the magnificence of His creation, in giving us His

son, and in the indwelling and inner witness of His Spirit. Our response to His love is unlike mixing cement which requires a one-time addition of water to complete the process. Our response to God's love is a life-long learning process. To respond we must do the inner work of responding to the examinations of our conscience, of practicing humility, of opening our hearts to God's love through daily prayer. The classic Beatles tune says, "All you need is Love!" and that is almost true; love must be put into action.

What is entirely true is that if you love God, if you love your neighbors and yourself with the proper healthy balance for each one, you will quickly build up a spiritual palace relationship with God. The life-long inner work is getting yourself to really love God as you should: that is putting your love for God, your neighbors and yourself into practice. Maybe it doesn't sound like it should be hard or require a lot of practice, but several factors, taken together, make it difficult to love God in the proper way (with all of your heart, mind, soul and strength). God's invisibility and subtleness in revealing himself, and the distance between us and God that God leaves to make room for us to have faith, all make it challenging for us to love God with all of our heart, mind, soul, and strength. Our natural desire for ego and physical gratification also make it difficult for us to love others as God would have us to, to approach them with a servants heart as Jesus instructed us to do (Matthew 20:25-28); and many things (such as our negative self-image) can make it difficult for us to love ourselves as we should. So just learning how to love God, neighbor, and self perfectly can be a life-long process.

One of the things about loving God that it took me many years to work through is that Jesus commandment to love God with all of our heart, mind soul and strength, isn't hyperbole, Jesus knew that the key to miraculous levels of interaction with God truly require us to love God with all of our heart, but that is so much easier said than done. "All of your heart" is a tremendous amount! I have discovered that it isn't just about love, "all of your heart" also means being completely open to God's will, yielded like Jesus washing Judas' feet; holding nothing we own or are back from God. That level of openness is a sort of radical openness to God that is generally, in my experience, born only from a time of pain and / or desperation.

Many of us have learned from losing in love over the years to harden our hearts or to protect our hearts from being hurt by not allowing ourselves to love whole heartedly. Many of us struggle with questions about God that prevent us from loving God wholeheartedly. Many have a log in our eye a giant blind spot about our own heart and either we love other people or things more than we love God. That was my struggle; I was convinced that I love God with all of my heart but it was only when I read a book on self-deception as a doctoral student, twenty-one years into my ministry that I realized the sad reality that I had not been willing to give up control over every part of my life. A love for God that holds things in reverse is not perfect love. I am still working to love others as I should, learning to grow past greed and be as generous as I should be, and past my too easy anger.

Since we recognize that God's love is the activating force for us to grow spiritually and to build our spiritual palace, what steps can we take, what can we do to increase our desire for God, our hunger to know and love and please God? The good news here is that since God already loves us with an amazing and perfect love (as the apostle John wrote in his first letter: "we love God because he first loved us"). When we want to grow in our love for God one of the easiest ways to do that is to become more aware of God's love working in us and in the people and the things around us. We need to put on "God glasses," and by that, I mean train ourselves to keep an eye out to look for God at work in the things and people around us. For example you might observe, "Why is Mr. Smith singing in the choir? It is obvious from his face that he is filled with the joy of the Lord." Seeing God in action is simply about paying closer attention to what is already happening.

Of course we can come to know God better and love God more by coming to church, by reading the Bible, and taking communion etc. and all these things help the foundation of our faith become stronger. A solid foundation is a source of strength and protection for us. In Proverbs 10 we read, "When the storms of life come, the wicked are whirled away, but the godly have a lasting foundation. (Proverbs 10:25 NLT) And we remember that Jesus said, "Those who come to me and listen to me and obey my teachings are like those who built their house on a solid rock and when the storms come that house will stand." A strong foundation is essential to building a spiritual palace that is truly a fortress of protection as well as a dwelling place of spiritual luxury.

Paul wrote to the Corinthians (1 Corinthians 12:3) that "no one can say "Jesus is Lord" except by the Holy Spirit." In other words if we believe in Jesus we believe because God has called us to and God has reached into us with the Holy Spirit to activate our faith. In the same way, if we feel called to build a spiritual palace relationship with God it is because God is calling us to do so, by the power of the Holy Spirit within us, and thanks be to God if we are responding to that call with faith. So we are blessed that God loves us, that God is calling us, and that God is working within us to build not just faith but a spiritual palace.

So if you have examined your conscience and you are approaching God with humility and with a sincere desire to know God better, to love God more, and to be pleasing to God, then your foundation is ready for your spiritual palace to be built.

Let us pray

> Lord, we give thanks and praise to You that Your creative power extends throughout the universe and that in the midst of all Your mighty creation You have placed us, nurtured us, and enabled us to be Your children; and have called us and enabled us to respond to Your love with our love for You. We ask Lord that you would give us eyes to see You in the people and things around us, that our knowledge of You would increase and our love for You would also increase. Strengthen us Lord by the power of the Holy Spirit within us to approach You and our life with humility and help us continually build up our spiritual palace relationship with You. Thank You Lord. We pray this in Jesus name.

Questions for Self-Reflection

- Have I made an examination of conscience?

- If so, do I feel the things I have identified are long term or short-term growth projects?

- How is my humility level?

- How strong is my desire to know God?

- To be pleasing to God?

- To love God as Jesus commanded?

Scripture Quotes Chapter Six
The Six Ingredients of Spiritual A Foundation
Originally preached 2/24/ 2019

https://www.youtube.com/watch?v=2-toqv_WV_Y

Isaiah 57:14-15 (NRSV) It shall be said, "Build up, build up, prepare the way, remove every obstruction from my people's way." For thus says the high and lofty one who inhabits eternity, whose name is Holy: <u>I dwell</u> in the high and holy place, and also <u>with those who are contrite and humble in spirit</u>, to revive the spirit of the humble, and to revive the heart of the contrite.

Luke 18:18-19 (NLT) Once a religious leader asked Jesus this question: "Good Teacher, what should I do to inherit eternal life?" 19"Why do you call me good?" Jesus asked him. "Only God is truly good.

Mark 10:43-45 But among you it will be different. Whoever wants to be a leader among you must be your servant, 44and whoever wants to be first among you must be the slave of everyone else. 45For even the Son of Man came not to be served but to serve others and to give his life as a ransom for many."

1 John 4:19 (TEV) [19]We love because God first loved us.

Genesis 2:7 (NRSV) [7]then the LORD God formed man from the dust of the ground and breathed into his nostrils the breath of life; and the man became a living being.

Proverbs 10:25 (NLT) When the storms of life come, the wicked are whirled away, but the godly have a lasting foundation.

Matthew 7:24-27 "Anyone who listens to my teaching and follows it is wise, like a person who builds a house on solid rock. 25Though the rain comes in torrents and the floodwaters rise and the winds beat against that house, it won't collapse because it is built on bedrock. 26But anyone who hears my teaching and ignores it is foolish, like a person who builds a house on sand. 27When the rains and floods come, and the winds beat against that house, it will collapse with a mighty crash."

1 Corinthians 12:3 (NRSV) ³Therefore I want you to understand that no one speaking by the Spirit of God ever says, "Let Jesus be cursed!" and <u>no one can say "Jesus is Lord" except by the Holy Spirit</u>.

(Luke 6:47-49 NLT) "When someone comes to me, listens to my teaching, and then follows it. It is like a person building a house who digs deep and lays the foundation on solid rock. When the floodwaters rise and break against the house, it stands firm because it is well built. But anyone who hears and doesn't obey is like a person who builds a house without a foundation. When the floods sweep down against that house, it will collapse into a heap of ruins."

1 Corinthians 3:10-17 ¹⁰Because of God's grace to me, I have laid the foundation like an expert builder. Now others are building on it. But whoever is building on this foundation must be very careful. ¹¹For <u>no one can lay any foundation other than the one we already have—Jesus Christ</u>. ¹²Anyone who builds on that foundation may use a variety of materials—gold, silver, jewels, wood, hay, or straw. ¹³But on the judgment day, fire will reveal what kind of work each builder has done. The fire will show if a person's work has any value. 14If the work survives, that builder will receive a reward. 15But if the work is burned up, the builder will suffer great loss. The builder will be saved, but like someone barely escaping through a wall of flames.

Isaiah 28:15-17 You boast, "We have struck a bargain to cheat death and have made a deal to dodge the grave. The coming destruction can never touch us, for <u>we have built a strong refuge</u>

made of lies and deception." Therefore, this is what the Sovereign LORD says: "Look! I am placing a foundation stone in Jerusalem, a firm and tested stone. It is a precious cornerstone that is safe to build on. Whoever believes need never be shaken. I will test you with the measuring line of justice and the plumb line of righteousness. Since your refuge is made of lies, a hailstorm will knock it down. Since it is made of deception, a flood will sweep it away.

Chapter Eight: Bricks & Mortar

Originally preached January 13, 2019

Now that we have done all the basics: we have our blueprints, construction wall, courtyard and foundation we are ready to start building up in earnest. Honestly if you have done the work of forming a vision; if you have entered into a covenant with God to seek excellence in your relationship; if you have made a commitment to your health in the process; and if you have done the things required to form a solid foundation, then you have truly done the majority of the hard work. From here on in you, "are being transformed into the same image (of Christ) from glory to glory, just as by the Spirit of the Lord" (2 Corinthians 3:17-18 NKJV). In other words from here on you are just adding blessing after blessing to your relationship with God. Not that you won't still have trials, troubles and tribulations – everyone has them. But you are in a covenant relationship with God, and God will be doing His part to protect you, guide you and bless you as you move through life. In this chapter I am going to talk about the basic building materials for building your spiritual palace. Before we get too much farther along, I want to invite you to join me in a prayer.

> Lord I thank You for the awesome privilege and responsibility of building a spiritual palace with You. May this chapter touch my heart, my mind and my spirit and help me in my desire to grow spiritually so that all I do, and desire will be acceptable to You, for You are my creator, my redeemer and my sustainer.

Billionaire industrialist and philanthropist Andrew Carnegie wrote: "Every act you have ever performed since the day you were born was because you wanted something. Aim for the highest and when it's a question of God's almighty spirit. Never say I can't." While we are all equally aiming for the highest heights, we may probably all picture something different and unique to us, however we all use the same basic building materials to build our spiritual palace. In any human relationship there is no substitute for time spent; any loving relationship depends on trust and honesty, and of course if you don't want it to happen it won't happen. The same things are true for our relationship with God. In constructing an earthly palace you need building materials such as metal, wood or stone; you need a frame to place those materials on and around; and you need the means to fasten or to affix the building materials to the frame. In the same way our spiritual palace requires building materials, a frame, and fasteners:

- Your building materials are your hours spent with God.

- The frame is your values system

- The fasteners or mortar is your desire for God.

- The Holy Spirit is your construction supervisor; He guides the entire construction process.

When the apostle Paul was talking about having the perfect relationship with God, he started by saying, "this one thing I do: forgetting what lies behind and straining forward to what lies ahead, I press on to possess that perfection for which Christ Jesus first possessed me..." And he ended with: "Let all who are spiritually mature agree on these things." What Paul seems to be saying here that building a perfect relationship with God is for those who are spiritually mature, i.e. those wish to move their faith from the basic, beginning levels to the highest levels up. Lastly, Paul encourages us towards spiritual maturity with these words: "My brothers and sisters in Christ, imitate me, follow my example, and aim to be among those who live up to this model." So Paul is asking and encouraging all of us to follow his example of pressing on towards the goal of perfection in our relationship with God.

I mentioned in the introduction of this book the health benefits that come to those who are active Christians. It is the application of your efforts to become mature spiritually, to seek perfection in your relationship with God, carried out over a number of years, that yield a huge benefit to your physical health as well. Your application of the Christian religion is more than just about the personal relationship between you God; it also about the ways that relationship shows up in your actions, including both your service to others in Christ name and your attending and being an active member of a church. Your attendance in church and your service to others in Christ name will help you build up your spiritual palace relationship with God and at the same time will help in reducing unhealthy blood pressure, it will strengthen your immune system, and help you fight off depression about as well as many drugs on the market.[1] The physical benefits of the practice of Christian faith are more evidence of God's infinite wisdom and knowledge: God knows you need a relatively healthy body to be able to worship God and relate to God, and your worshipping and relating to God strengthens your body's health so that you can worship and relate with God, and so that you can better enjoy the blessings of life on this planet. It is that old upward reinforcing cycle rearing its beautiful head again.

There is an old saying: "Happy wife, happy life." As a person who is in love with his wife after 37 years of marriage, I have learned that in our relationship there is no substitute for time. Every single day I spend time speaking with her, listening to what is on her mind; letting her know that I appreciate her and love her; and I make plans for regular extra time as well, weekly

---

[1] Moll, Rob. The Surprising Links Between Faith and Health 5 ways your faith improves your health.
https://relevantmagazine.com/life/surprising-links-between-faith-and-health
Posted On November 3, 2014.

date night, walks together, etc. The result is a very close loving relationship.

The same criteria hold true for our relationship with God, our loving relationship with God is built up through daily communication and taking extra time each week as well. The building materials of a spiritual palace are the hours you spent with God in worship, in prayer, in service, in Bible reading, and if I have left anything out, in any God related activity. Each hour you spend on some activity involving your relationship with God is another brick, another stone, another plank for your palace. Singing in the choir, working at the church rummage sale, taking care of a shut-in, cooking for the homeless, vacuuming the sanctuary, personal fitness, anything done with the intention of pleasing God is another brick or plank in the wall.

The key is you have to be doing it for God: since I was a kid singing in the choir I have known and observed many people over the years that come to church every Sunday but don't know God at all. Many people come to church strictly to get their, "I'm a good person card" punched. Their bodies are in church but their hearts and filled with anger and hatred, and other negatives. God knows what is in your mind (psalm 139:2) and in your heart (Psalm 17:3), so if you are not doing it for God, he knows it. Your time in worship, in service to others, in prayer, in Bible study; it has to be about God, about trying to grow in knowledge, in love, in devotion to God. Jesus told the story of the Pharisee and the sinner standing and praying in the temple, the sinner said, "Lord, have mercy on me I am a terrible sinner!" and the Pharisee said, "Thank God I'm not like that guy!" Jesus said it was the sinner who went home forgiven (Luke 18:10-14). God knows the contents of our hearts and that is what matter to him. Even prayer can be empty and meaningless if your mind is elsewhere. Praying the rosary can be a spiritual growth tool if you think about the meaning of each word you are saying as you pray, or it can be as empty and useless as reading the phone book if you mindlessly repeat the formula prayer over and over to accomplish a set number of repetitions.

If you think about all the hours you have spent attending church over the years, all the hours in prayer, in service, in study, everything you have done with the intention of being pleasing to God; you may have accumulated a huge pile of bricks. Have you been using them to build up your spiritual palace? Unfortunately, some people are sitting on a big pile of bricks, but they never build a spiritual palace, because they haven't got a vision for it, they never thought about building towards perfection or excellence, or they never realized that is possible. Others don't build because they don't ever make a framework to build on.

The framework of our spiritual palace is our value system, which includes our personal integrity, and our compassion towards others. Paul writes: "Since God chose you to be the holy people he loves, you must clothe yourselves with compassion, tenderhearted mercy, kindness, humility, gentleness, and patience" (Colossians 3:12 NRSV). We must cloth ourselves with compassion, means love for others being reflected by our actions all the time. The apostle James wrote:

> **James 2:14-17 (NLT)** [14]What good is it, dear brothers and sisters, if you say you have faith but don't show it by your actions? Can that kind of faith save anyone? [15]Suppose you see a brother or sister who has no food or clothing, [16]and you say, "Good-bye and have a good day; stay warm and eat well"—but then you don't give that person any food or clothing. What good does that do? [17]So you see, faith by itself isn't enough. Unless it produces good deeds, it is dead and useless.

I don't know if you know this, but in some circles Christians have a bad reputation for hypocrisy; we are known for talking a good talk but not walking a good walk, for doing exactly what James warned us not to do; basically having passion for God without compassion for God's children.

Compassion or caring towards others is an essential key to an excellent relationship with God. True compassion for others includes the other things Paul mentioned: tenderhearted mercy, kindness, humility, gentleness, and patience. When I prayed to ask God what I should say you about how to build up your compassion for others, God's answer was surprising. "The only way to increase your level of compassion for others is to grow in your love for yourself as a child of God. Only when you love yourself as God intends that you do can you also truly love others."

The New Testament was originally written in Greek, and in the Greek language there are three different words for love: eros or romantic love, philia or the love of a brother, and agape or Christian love. Loving yourself in this sense is the "agape" love that you may have heard of. Agape or Christian love is to love another person as a child of God. While you can love others if you don't love yourself, your love will be not truly healthy, either for you or for the person you love or both. Jesus said that if we want to be forgiven, we must forgive others (Matthew 6:15), and that includes ourselves. If we have unresolved anger at ourselves that anger will spill over and at least slightly taint the love, we have diminishing what we are able to offer to others.

In my first semester of Divinity School I was hired as student Associate Pastor of Trinity Avenue Presbyterian, a fairly large church in downtown Durham. My first Sunday on the job I had never so much as read a prayer in leading a church before and I was given the assignment to lead a responsive reading of Psalm 24. With the over confidence of an ivy league graduate student I didn't bother to read the psalm beforehand, but in spite of my confidence in reading the words with excellence I was not so confident about standing up before the large congregation. I was nervous and my hands were like ice. I thought "I will go run my hands under hot water and when my hands are warm, I will be relaxed." So I stood there at the men's room sink for about five minutes with my hands under hot running water. They did warm up and it was time to head out into the sanctuary. I opened the hymnal and led the congregation: "Who can stand before the Lord?" I asked. The congregation responded, "He who has clean hands and a pure heart!" I thanked God for that bit of comic relief, that certainly seemed like a blessing that God cooked up just for me.

Clean hands and *pure hearts* is a metaphorical way of saying - a person who is honest and has personal integrity in all their dealings with others. The Bible makes it clear that honesty and integrity are essential to God. In Proverbs we read: "The Lord hates liars but is pleased with those who keep their word" (12:22 TEV). Deuteronomy tells us God is, "A God of Truth" (32:4) so God is all about honesty by his very nature. Integrity means scrupulous attention to honesty in words and your dealings with others; the Old Testament also calls that *righteousness*. The book of Proverbs tells us: "The way of the LORD is a fortress to those with integrity, but it destroys the wicked." And "The LORD detests people with crooked hearts, but he delights in those with integrity." Why does God hate lying and delight in those with integrity? Because dishonesty is the exact opposite of God. Satan is the opposite of God, and Jesus called him, "The father of lies." Whether we are lying to ourselves or to others lying is destructive almost all the time and God is about building us up not tearing us down.

King David is quoted in 1 Chronicles praying: "I know, my God, that you examine our hearts and rejoice when you find integrity there." I don't want to hammer this too hard (to borrow a construction metaphor) but integrity is essential to the framework of your whole spiritual palace: just as you can never build a spiritual palace if you are not compassionate towards others, so too you cannot build a relationship with God on dishonesty, you must be committed to honesty. The hours we spend in prayer, in Bible reading, in worship and in service, when laid over a foundation of commitment to God, and wrapped around a framework of honesty and integrity make for the building of a very secure spiritual dwelling.

I think we probably all know someone who has a good moral framework – who is honest in their dealings with others, and who is compassionate towards others but they have no bricks: they have never spent any time building up their relationship with God through prayer or worship or study or service in his name. My grandfather Dr. Walter Ehrlich was a great example: he was a very good and honest man, a family doctor who was not in medicine for the money but to help people, but no relationship with God. His attitude towards life was, "Love is the highest good" and his hero was Albert Schweitzer who taught that we should revere all life. Dr. Ehrlich loved helping people, but he rejected God because of his combat experiences in WW1 and with the Nazis in WW2. I am glad that shortly before he died, we had a long conversation about God, and he said that for the first time he opened his mind to the possibility of the reality of God. I am confident that God judged him by the content of his character and his life of service, but I feel very bad for him because he missed out on a close personal relationship with God - the most wonderful thing life has to offer.

Lastly, maybe you know some people as I do, who don't build a spiritual palace even though they believe in God and have a good moral frame and a sizeable pile of bricks; but they still don't build a spiritual palace because they lack the fasteners, I mean they don't have a strong desire for God. The commitment to serve God and to develop an excellent relationship with God must be married to a passion for God. By passion I mean you must be hungry to know God and experience God's love. Your desire for God is the glue, the mortar, the fasteners that holds the whole construction project together. Without a strong desire for God the construction will never occur. Interestingly the prophet Ezekiel pointed out the same thing: that if the mortar you use on your building is weak then when the storms come your building will collapse.

> **Ezekiel 13:10-16 (NKJV)** ¹⁰"Because, indeed, because they have seduced My people, saying, 'Peace!' when *there is* no peace—and one builds a wall, and they plaster it with untempered *mortar*— ¹¹say to those who plaster *it* with untempered *mortar,* that it will fall... ¹³Therefore thus says the Lord GOD: "I will cause a stormy wind to break forth in My fury; and there shall be a flooding rain in My anger, and great hailstones in fury to consume *it.*

In this case the untempered or bad mortar Ezekiel is talking is a metaphor for the faulty and false teaching by fake prophets who have told the people of Israel that they don't need to repent and return to God because their nation is secure. Ezekiel's metaphor is aimed at a different target, but the principle of the metaphor is the same: if the mortar, the glue, the fasteners are bad then the building you are building will not stand up to the storms of life. Our desire for God helps hold us together in tough times even when our faith is not strong. Since our desire for God is the essential glue which holds our entire building project together how do we go about increasing our desire for God?

Increasing our desire for God is a work of the Holy Spirit; our job is to invite the Holy Spirit in and then get out His way, (which unfortunately we often fail at spectacularly). Most of us don't have much of a clue about how the Holy Spirit works. I have been a Christian for 44 years and a pastor for 35 years and

I feel like it was only in the last five years that I really feel I understand the Holy Spirit. As an example of the complexities of the Holy Spirit, I mentioned in the beginning of the chapter that the Holy Spirit is the construction supervisor. By that I mean that when we have put ourselves in God's hands and we have been doing everything right we still need the help of God to progress. The Holy Spirit opens doors for us and guides us by providing clear signs.

Proverbs 3:6 tells us, "Seek his will in all you do, and he will show you which path to take" (NLT). That is not a metaphor it is a reality, God truly gives us signs and opens doors, but you will never discover the truth of that until you trust God for that and put yourself in His hands. The Holy Spirit also gives us wisdom and discernment, but we need to remember that God wants us to do for ourselves what we can do, and that includes in this case reading the Wisdom literature in the Bible, particularly Proverbs, Psalms, Ecclesiastes and Job.

Since desire for God is crucial to developing our relationship with God, and since desire for God is the same as being hungry for God, you can increase your hunger for God in a way similar to increasing your bodily hunger – work up an appetite, by exercising. Spiritual exercises are different types of prayers and meditations designed to help you feel the presence of God. Feeling the presence of God then leads you to want more of the same making you hungry for God. The interesting paradox of the Holy Spirit is that when you receive it, it fills you with peace and joy, but, at the same time it creates in you an unquenchable desire to remain filled with the Holy Spirit. In all honesty the desire to be filled with the Holy Spirit is an addiction, but unlike earthly addictions which tend to lead to us into ill health and even destruction, addiction to the Holy Spirit leads us to greater health and satisfaction with life.

King Solomon prayed for Godly desire on behalf of the people of Israel, "May the LORD our God... give us the desire to do his will in everything and to obey all the commands, decrees, and regulations that he gave our ancestors" (1 Kings 8:57-58 NLT). Desiring God means that you want to please God, to know God, and to experience God. Jesus promised us if we pray for the Holy Spirit God will give us the Spirit, "If you then, who are evil, know how to give good gifts to your children, how much more will the heavenly Father give the Holy Spirit to those who ask him (Luke 11:13 NRSV). So at the end of this chapter I have included a spiritual exercise for increasing your compassion for others, and another exercise to increase desire for God, and a prayer to ask God for the Holy Spirit.

I want to close the chapter with this thought: from Psalm 63 which notes the joys of relationship with God, "My soul is satisfied as with a rich feast, and my mouth praises you with joyful lips when I think of you on my bed, and meditate on you in the watches of the night." One of the main purposes of this book is to increase your level of joy until the words of the 23rd psalm become a reality to you: "my cup runneth over!"

While the process of building a spiritual palace is a lifelong adventure the good news about the process is that God does allow some shortcuts. God's shortcuts come in the form of miracles. Miracles are the experience of something happening that either could not happen in nature or be explained by natural laws, or that the unusualness and timing of the event is so amazingly and against such long odds and with such benefit to the individual or individuals involved as to indicate it is the action of a loving, all-knowing supernatural being. For example Jesus healed two blind men by touching their eyes (Matt. 9:27-29). When you have a miraculous experience of or with God, if you unpack it (take time to understand its implications) you can leapfrog ahead in your spiritual growth. One miracle can be worth more than one year of going to church every Sunday.

I hope and pray that God will allow you to access the short cut of a miracle, and I assure you that in time if your heart is right with God, and you are hungry for God you will open the door to the miraculous. An open door is not a guarantee, God does not function like a cosmic vending machine – put in the right prayer coin and out pops your miracle – but a heart right with God is the precondition.

Before moving on to the next chapter let's take a few minutes to pray together, and then I invite you to take a few more minutes to do the spiritual exercises.

A Prayer for the Holy Spirit

I thank You God my Father and Jesus Christ my Lord for giving us Your Holy Spirit and everything we need, to live in Your presence. All love, praise, honor, glory, joy and thanks to You Holy Spirit: for You are Lord God present with us, in us and around us. Thank You for coming to me through my faith in Jesus, and resting inside me, cleansing me, filling me, giving me many spiritual gifts, especially the gift of faith. Lord God – Father - please help me base myself in your Spirit so that I do not sin against You in any way this day and the next 24 hours, or until I pray to You again. Please surround me with Your Spirit so that I do not go in any direction you do not want physically, emotionally or spiritually, and please cover me with Your Holy Spirit and protect me from anyone or anything that would do me harm, and please let Your Holy Spirit rest on me and fill me so that I may be filled with Your light and peace and joy and so that I may be your light, Your joy, Your peace for those I come in contact with this day.

An Exercise to Increase Compassion

This spiritual exercise was inspired by the spiritual exercises of St. Ignatius. The aim of this exercise is to contemplate the love God has for you that is made clear in the suffering that Jesus went through for you. At the start of his book of spiritual exercises Ignatius wrote several annotations two of which are very relevant to us and paraphrased below:

Annotation. The first Annotation is that by Spiritual Exercises I mean ways of examining one's conscience, of meditating, of contemplating, of praying vocally and mentally, and of performing other spiritual actions, that result in experiences and feelings that strengthen our spirituality. In the same way that you can exercise physically and build up your muscles you can also exercise spiritually the result is greater understanding of and closeness too God our creator.

Annotation. A person is busy with the affairs of life or of business, requires only half an hour daily to exercise him or herself spiritually.

Annotation. The more desperate for God we are the more apt we are to approach and to reach our Creator and Lord, and to receive His Divine graces and gifts. We are never closer to God than when we are broken hearted.

Begin with prayer: (With eyes closed in a secluded spot)

Lord God, in your love for me and for the world you sent your son to be our teacher, example, and when the time was right, to be the offering for our sins. Lord God, in this exercise help us contemplate the suffering of Christ and help us to feel a measure of what he felt that we might be moved with compassion for him.

The Exercise: Imagine you are on the scene in Jerusalem as Jesus is standing with hands bound with rope in front of him, standing before Pilate who is seated under the portico at the end of a large courtyard. You are standing nearby, only Jesus can see you. Pilate, who wants to let Jesus go has been arguing with the priests who want him crucified. He gives up and says, "I shall have him flogged", and he waves his hand. The guards lead Jesus to the paved military parade ground that is next to Pilate's palace. In front of a large gathering of soldiers he is stripped of his robe and tied to a tall wooden frame in the shape of a square. You watch as ropes are tied around his wrists and used to pull his arms up and out in a "Y" shape his feet are just barely touching the ground. With a whip made of a long wooden handle with three leather straps attached to the end of it, and at the end of each strap a lead weight is attached; the whipping beings. A soldier counts out loud as Jesus receives 39 lashes on his back then 39 more split between his chest and the backs of his legs. You stand nearby, invisible, watching helplessly as each lash cuts into his skin; each lash bringing him one cut for each of the lead weights at the ends of the three lashes. Jesus does not call out, but each lash causes him to breathe out loudly.

PAUSE NOW TO VISUALIZE THE SCENE: With your eyes closed, what would you see as you look around, what would you hear? Smell? Feel?

At last the whipping is done. The take release him from the frame and ties his hands together again, they make him sit on a stool. One soldier has been making a crown of thorns while they whipped him. They place it on his head and smash it down with wooden rods. They throw a purple cloth around his shoulders (a sign of royalty or rank), and they bow down to him and mock him saying "Hail to the King of the Jews." They strip off the cape and allow him the dignity of putting his own robe back on. One soldier at each side they help him walk back through the parade ground to Pilate.

You walk behind and stand invisible next to Pilate. Pilate says to crowd "Behold the man!" He means to show that Jesus has been thoroughly punished. He is hoping that will satisfy the crowd, but they call out "Crucify Him!" Pilate says, "Would you have me crucify your king?" The crowd responds, "We have no king but Caesar!" and continue yelling out for his crucifixion. Pilate gives in and orders the crucifixion. With Jesus standing there Pilate orders a pitcher of water and a bowl. One servant holds the bowl another pours water over Pilate's hands – He says, "I wash my hands of his death." And he tells the guards "Crucify him."

PAUSE NOW TO VISUALIZE THE SCENE: With your eyes closed, what would you see as you look around, what would you hear? Smell? Feel?

Jesus is made to walk through the narrow city streets, carrying a wooden cross. He is weak from the whipping and stumbles and falls several times. The guards frustrated with his slow pace grab a man from the crown and force his to carry the cross. The journey from Pilate to up to the top of a little hill just outside the walls of the city is less than a half mile. At the top the hill the cross is laid on the ground and Jesus is made to lay on it. His hands and feet are tied to the cross to hold them in place as the nails are driven into place, the ropes are removed, and the cross is stood up the end dropped into a hole in rock. It is now about 9 a.m. the sun is shining but clouds start gathering. The sky darkens but it is small relief to Jesus, sweat and blood mix on his forehead, and run down his arms and chest. You stand before him looking up at him. He alternates back and forth periodically between the agony of standing on nailed feet which allows him to breath freely or hanging from nailed palms which makes breathing difficult. He looks at you and says "I am suffering this so you may know that your sins are forgiven. You are now made acceptable to God as his child so that may have freedom from fear in this life and a place in God's house in eternity." With that he looks up and says, "Father, into your hands I commit my spirit." And He dies.

PAUSE NOW TO VISUALIZE THE SCENE: With your eyes closed, what would you see as you look around, what would you hear? Smell? Feel? What do you feel emotionally?

Close with a prayer:

Thank God for sending Jesus to die for us and thank You Jesus for being willing to die so painfully for us. Lord God, you are the creator of all people and You want all people to be Your children. Lord, I thank You for Your love for me: I love You, and I want to love the others that You have called to also be Your children. Help me grow daily in my awareness of how much You love me and each one of your children that You sent Jesus to die for. Lord fill me with love and compassion for all of Your creations, and even more for the others of Your creation, who You have called to be my brothers and sisters, my fellow children of Yours through Jesus Christ our Lord.

Exercise to Increase Desire for the Lord by Being Filled with the Joy of the Lord

1. **Center** - take a few minutes to relax and think of God. Pray the Lord's Prayer twice – thinking about the meaning of the words.

2. **Ask** – "God, Father, Son & Holy Spirit, please be with me now, give me strength and wisdom, help me to know what things are on my mind and keeping me from being filled with joy. Thank you, Lord!"

3. **Think** – After asking God what things in you are blocking out the feeling of being filled with joy, things should start coming to your mind, fears, worries, doubts, etc. One at a time name each one - and one at a time lift it up to God: "Lord I sense that I am feeling (for example) fear of failure (or for

example) I am feeling doubt about your reality and it is weighing on me and keeping me from feeling joyful."

4. **Bind** – Name whatever it is and use this formula to get rid of it: "Fear of failure (or whatever it is that you have identified) holding me down, in the name of the Father Son, and Holy Spirit I bind you with the Holy Spirit" (picture the holy spirit totally wrapped around it).

5. **Cast out** – "Fear of failure, in the name of God the Father, Christ the Son and the Holy Spirit I cast you out of me! Be gone from me and don't return!"

6. **Heal** – "Lord, fill me with Your Holy Spirit. Touch me with Your Holy Spirit in all the places where fear of failure held on to me. Heal those places and cover them with Your Spirit so that fear may not find this place to hold on again."

7. **Give thanks** – "I thank you and praise You Lord for healing me and filling me with Your Holy Spirit. Praise You Lord! Thank You Lord! Alleluia! Amen!"

8. **Repeat** - (generally, the first time you do this exercise there will be more than one thing keeping you from being filled with joy, so repeat 1-7 until you feel lighter.) It can take as much as 1/2 and hour to an hour to surface all the things that are buried in your subconscious mind and keeping you from being filled with Joy.

Building a Spiritual Palace Part 3: Bricks & Mortar
January 13, 2019

2 Corinthians 3:17-18 (NKJV) ¹⁷Now the Lord is the Spirit; and where the Spirit of the Lord *is,* there *is* liberty. ¹⁸But we all, with unveiled face, beholding as in a mirror the glory of the Lord, are being transformed into the same image <u>from glory to glory</u>, just as by the Spirit of the Lord.

Philippians 3:12-16 (NLT) 12I don't mean to say that I have already achieved these things or that I have already reached perfection. But <u>I press on to possess that perfection</u> for which Christ Jesus first possessed me. No, dear brothers and sisters, I have not achieved it, but I focus on this one thing: <u>Forgetting the past and looking forward to what lies ahead,</u> 14I press on to reach the end of the race and receive the heavenly prize for which God, through Christ Jesus, is calling us. <u>Let all who are spiritually mature agree on these things.</u> If you disagree on some point, I believe God will make it plain to you. 16But we must hold on to the progress we have already made. My Brothers and sisters in Christ, <u>imitate me, follow my example, and aim to be among those who live up to this model</u>.

Luke 18:10-14 (NLT) 10"Two men went to the Temple to pray. One was a Pharisee, and the other was a despised tax collector. 11The Pharisee stood by himself and prayed this prayer: 'I thank you, God, that I am not a sinner like everyone else. For I don't cheat, I don't sin, and I don't commit adultery. I'm certainly not like that tax collector! 12I fast twice a week, and I give you a tenth of my income.'

13"But the tax collector stood at a distance and dared not even lift his eyes to heaven as he prayed. Instead, he beat his chest in sorrow, saying, 'O God, be merciful to me, for I am a sinner.' 14I tell you, this sinner, not the Pharisee, returned home justified before God. For those who exalt themselves will be humbled, and those who humble themselves will be exalted."

Colossians 3:12 (NLT) 12Since God chose you to be the holy people he loves, <u>you must clothe yourselves with compassion, tenderhearted mercy, kindness, humility, gentleness, and patience</u>.

James 2:14-17 (NLT) ¹⁴What good is it, dear brothers and sisters, if you say you have faith but don't show it by your actions? Can that kind of faith save anyone? ¹⁵Suppose you see a brother or sister who has no food or clothing, 16and you say, "Good-bye and have a good day; stay warm and eat well"—but then you don't give that person any food or clothing. What good does that do? ¹⁷So you see, faith by itself isn't enough. Unless it produces good deeds, it is dead and useless.

Psalms 24:3 - 4 (NRSV) And who shall stand in his holy place? ⁴Those who have **clean** hands and pure hearts, who do not lift up their souls to what is false, and do not swear deceitfully.

Deuteronomy 32:4 (NKJV) He *is* the Rock, His work *is* perfect; For all His ways *are* justice, A God of truth and without injustice; Righteous and upright *is* He.

Proverbs 10:29 (NLT) The way of <u>the LORD is a fortress to those with integrity</u>, but it destroys the wicked.

Proverbs 11:20 The LORD <u>detests people with crooked hearts</u>, but he <u>delights in those with integrity</u>.

Proverbs 6:16-19 (TMSG) Here are six things God hates, and one more that he loathes with a passion… eyes that are arrogant, a tongue that lies, 19a mouth that lies under oath…

John 8:44 (NRSV) 44You are from your father the devil, and you choose to do your father's desires. He was a murderer from the beginning and does not stand in the truth, because there is no truth in him. When he lies, he speaks according to his own nature, for he is a liar and the <u>father of lies</u>.

1 Chronicles 29:17 (NLT) I know, my God, that you examine our hearts and rejoice when you find integrity there. You know I have done all this with good motives, and I have watched your people offer their gifts willingly and joyously.

Ezekiel 13:10-16 (NKJV) "Because, indeed, because they have seduced My people, saying, 'Peace!' when *there is* no peace—and one builds a wall, and they plaster it with untempered *mortar*— [11]say to those who plaster *it* with untempered *mortar*, that it will fall...[13]Therefore thus says the Lord GOD: "I will cause a stormy wind to break forth in My fury; and there shall be a flooding rain in My anger, and great hailstones in fury to consume *it*.

1 Kings 8:57-58 (NLT) 57May the LORD our God be with us as he was with our ancestors; may he never leave us or abandon us. 58May he gives us the desire to do his will in everything and to obey all the commands, decrees, and regulations that he gave our ancestors.

Luke 11:13 (NRSV) If you then, who are evil, know how to give good gifts to your children, how much more will the heavenly Father give the Holy Spirit to those who ask him!"
Psalms 63:5-7 (NRSV) My soul is satisfied as with a rich feast, and my mouth praises you with joyful lips when I think of you on my bed, and meditate on you in the watches of the night;

Matthew 9:27-30 (NLT) [27]After Jesus left the girl's home, two blind men followed along behind him, shouting, "Son of David, have mercy on us!" [28]They went right into the house where he was staying, and Jesus asked them, "Do you believe I can make you see?" "Yes, Lord," they told him, "we do." [29]Then he touched their eyes and Said, "Because of your faith, it will happen." [30]Then their eyes were opened, and they could see! Jesus sternly warned them, "Don't tell anyone about this."

Chapter Nine: The Dining Room

Originally Preached March 10, 2019

This chapter is entitled *The Dining Room* because I want to talk about the importance of continually feeding ourselves spiritually, as we either are under construction or already living in a spiritual palace. Feeding ourselves daily spiritually is as important to our spiritual health as eating food daily is important to our physical health. Napoleon Bonaparte, according to Wikipedia, led armies in 72 battles and was victorious 68 times so I would say he qualifies as an expert when he said, "An army marches on its stomach." Are we not members of the army of God? And if we are going to be effective Christians, if we are going to be successful in building up a relationship with God that is truly a spiritual palace, then we too must be well fed on good and plentiful spiritual food.

In this chapter I am going to talk about how we can feed our spirit for the journey, for the battles that we are in or that we will be in, in our future. Before I begin, I want to open with a prayer.

Let Us Pray:

> Thank you, God, for opportunity this chapter gives to explore together the potentials and avenues for a higher and more blessed way of living. Be with us now as we are reading and writing, so that all that is written and read will be acceptable in Your sight, for You are our Creator, our Redeemer and our Sustainer. Thank You God!

For the research project I did for my doctoral dissertation I interviewed the fifteen most successful pastors out of the more than seven-hundred Methodist pastors in the Florida Annual Conference. My plan was to try and find some characteristics they all have in common I so that I could share that information with the Annual Conference to help them help other pastors be more successful. What I expected to find in my research, my original hypothesis, was that the number one unifying factor that all these highly successful pastors had in common would prove to be that they all experienced many miracles, and that they were empowered for ministry by being spiritually fed by and sustained by these miraculous experiences.

What I discovered instead was that while several of them had experienced multiple miracles, several others never experienced any or no more than one significant miraculous event. But I did find a commonality among them all: they are all exceptionally good at feeding their souls in other ways. They also had other three other things in common: all fifteen were also all intentional about taking care of their temple of the Holy Spirit (their body) by exercising regularly, generally at least twice every week. They all take good care of their emotions, through establishing some kind of an emotional support network for themselves; and they all take care of their minds by reading a lot, mostly non-fiction.

As I was interviewing these pastors a surprising picture quickly emerged from the data – it was how often they all fed themselves spiritually daily and the quantity of food for their spirit they were consuming every day. I thought to myself, "These pastors are spiritual gluttons! If these pastors fed themselves every day physically as they did spiritually, they would all weigh six-hundred pounds!" It was a complete reversal of my expectations: instead of being driven from the outside (miraculous experiences), they were driven from the inside, empowered for ministry by feeding themselves spiritually all day long, using a variety of spiritual foods, including prayer, reading the Bible, meditation, Christian conversation, and being very intentional about looking for and discerning God at work in the people and things around them. What I learned from these pastors is that a spiritual palace relationship can be rapidly built up if we concentrate on feeding ourselves spiritually every day.

In his letter the Hebrews Paul talked about our need to feed on spiritual food: "<u>You are like babies</u> who need milk and cannot eat solid food… Solid food is for those who are mature, who through training have the skill to recognize the difference between right and wrong." Solid spiritual food is for those who are mature Christians that is, those who have prepared the ground in their hearts and minds by examining their conscience, and confessing and repenting of that which does not belong (as I spoke about in Chapter Five); and who have laid down a foundation of having the right attitude towards God and towards ourselves (as I spoke about in Chapter six); and who are intentional, committed and consistent in their desire for God (as I spoke about in Chapter Seven).

In Psalm 23, verse five says of God, "You prepare a table before me…" That is the New King James Version; the New Living Translation and most modern translations say something like this: "You prepare a feast for me…" Jesus also spoke, in Matthew's Gospel (8:11), about a feast in heaven prepared for those of faith. If you picture a fancy dining room in a palace, and how large and impressive that is you might also envision that if God is preparing a table for you the spiritual food we are going to have in your spiritual palace will be a feast – worthy of a palace, and you would be correct. However, a terrific spiritual feast does not necessarily mean that it is particularly fancy or gourmet.

Never-the-less, God must be a great chef - when God provided food to sustain the Israelites in the desert what He gave them was manna, and on occasion, quail. The manna was apparently so good that they consumed it daily for 40 years, so it must have been delicious and nutritious. When Jesus fed the 5000 again a very simple meal, he gave them only fish and bread. The spiritual food the Lord provides for us like that - simple and basic. It is more varied than just fish and bread but still pretty simple.

The first course in God's feast is knowledge: to know God, and to know that you are known by God, is an absolute feast for your soul (I will talk more about how to increase your knowledge of God further on in the chapter and devote an entire chapter to it *The Throne Room*). In Proverbs we read, "Fear of the LORD is the foundation of true knowledge" (Proverbs 1:7 NLT). Fear in this verse means both fear in the sense of being at least a little afraid; and also to revere and desire to please or obey. The first thing that happens when you spend time trying to get to know God is you begin to realize the power of God as creator and sustainer of the universe. To know God is to realize the infinity of God and the omniscience of God, and that knowledge has to engender at least a little bit of fear as we contemplate our mortality and size compared to the eternity and infinity of God.

The heavenly feast also includes a delicious portion of assurance. Paul, in his letter to the Romans talked about the Holy Spirit bearing witness, giving us assurance, that we are children of God. If we are lucky enough to be blessed to have the experience of feeling the power and / or the presence of the Holy Spirit and have the Holy Spirit "testify" inside us that is a spiritual gift – known as the gift of assurance. To know that you are accepted by God as a child of His is a rich feast for your soul.

What feast table would be complete without bread? What feast would not include wine? Jesus said that he himself is the bread of life and the real drink. He said,

> "I am the bread of life! 49Your ancestors ate manna in the wilderness, but they all died. 50Anyone who eats the bread from heaven, however, will never die. 51I am the living bread that came down from heaven. Anyone who eats this bread will live forever; and this bread, which I will offer so the world may live, is my flesh." (John 6:48-52)
>
> Jesus said to them, "I am telling you the truth: if you do not eat the flesh of the Son of Man and drink his blood, you will not have life in yourselves. ⁵⁴Those who eat my flesh and drink my blood have eternal life, and I will raise them to life on the last day. ⁵⁵For my flesh is the real food; my blood is the real drink. ⁵⁶Those who eat my flesh and drink my blood live in me, and I live in them. John 6:53-56 (TEV)

It is a difficult saying to take in at first; John tells us (6:60) "many of Jesus followers heard this and said, "This teaching is too hard. Who can listen to it?" But what Jesus is saying is that believing in him is like eating a spiritual meal from heaven that, when we eat it, or in other words when we believe in him, it will feed us eternal life. In his first letter to the Corinthians Paul says something similar: "<u>When we bless the cup at the Lord's Table, aren't we sharing in the blood of Christ? And when we break the bread, aren't we sharing in the body of Christ?</u>" (1 Corinthians 10:16 NLT). So taking communion is a great way to feed yourself spiritually, but Paul also warned us in that same letter (11:27-29) that taking communion is only effective for us if our heart is right with God, and if we take it with our hearts and minds in the wrong place it actually will not only do us no good, but it will do us harm.

When Jesus was being tempted by Satan, he responded to the temptation to turn stones into bread by telling Satan, "Man does not live by bread alone but by every word that comes from the mouth of God" (Matthew 4:3-4). From that passage pastors often talk about, "feeding on the word" by which they mean reading the Bible as spiritual food. Just like with communion, if your heart and mind are not right with God, you can read the Bible all you want, and it will not feed you spiritually. An open mind is required to receive the highest level of spiritual benefit from the scriptures – by that I mean scrupulous intellectual honesty and a willingness to go wherever the truth leads. Some or perhaps it is more accurate to say many scholars read the Bible as entirely a manmade book; they are closed the very concept that God or a spiritual intelligent force might have influenced its writing. At most they will call it, "a manmade book on which you can see the fingerprints of God." A smaller number of scholars, and I include myself in their number would say the Bible is "a God-made book on which you can see the fingerprints of the human authors."

To God intellectual honesty is as important as any other type of honesty. God is not afraid of skeptical inquiry. Intellectual honesty means being open to going wherever the truth leads and being willing to consider any rational argument. Intellectual honesty also means applying scrupulous unbiased research before concluding. Some critics focus only on the violence of some parts of the Old Testament and they argue that God is a blood thirsty tyrant. That is not intellectual honesty; it is like a blind person only able to feel one part of an elephant trying to describe the whole animal. The totality of the Bible as well as the historical context of the time and setting in which it was written all need to be considered. The effects of reading the Bible on believers' lives can also be measured.

Intellectual honesty and scrupulous research will lead you to the conclusion that the reality of God can now be established mathematically based on statistical probabilities and the physics of the big bang and the resultant weak, strong, and electromagnetic forces and gravity. The divine authorship of the

Bible is not able to be proven in the same way. Believers point to examples of fulfilled prophesies, such as the alignment of the events of the crucifixion of Jesus with Psalm 22; but skeptics claim it was revisionism, that the gospel writers added details to the crucifixion narrative to make it jive with Psalm 22. So the authenticity of the Bible is a matter of faith, however this becomes a case of "believing is seeing." It is only when your mind is truly open to the possibility of the reality of God and the holiness of the Bible that you can begin to sense the presence of the Holy Spirit as you are reading the Bible. God will not kick down the doors and force His way into your mind, or to your heart; you need to open the doors if you want the king of glory to come in. That is true for the Holy Spirit, for faith in Christ and for accessing the divine through reading scripture; it only becomes food for your soul when you are open to it being so.

Now the highly successful pastors who I interviewed all not only had their hearts and minds open to God, they all made a practice of feeding their spirit by continually looking for God at work in the people and things around them. That is the most valuable lesson I learned from them in my research – to look for the divine in the people and things around me more. They didn't just see a greeter standing at the door of church or a choir member; they saw God at work in that person, and the person responding to the love of God. They didn't just see a sunset they saw God's creativity at work; and this way of looking at the people and things around them made them feel love for God, and God's love for them. In looking for God at work in the people and things around them they saw God in these places, and it fed their souls.

Iyanla Vanzant, New York Times Best-Selling Author writes this:

> "Are you aware that your spirit needs to be fed? Did you know that your spirit would be

> delighted to partake in a feast of spiritual food? How about a plate full of prayer? Or maybe a few hours of succulent self-reflection. Perhaps a piping-hot selection of spiritual literature, served by the side of a lake or under a tree, would satisfy your spiritual hunger. Can you imagine feasting for a few hours on spiritually uplifting music? What about some forgiveness à la mode, topped with compassion? You cannot imagine how much your spirit would enjoy it.

The last part of the spiritual meal, I guess we can call it dessert, is fruit - the fruit of the Spirit which Paul says is love, joy, peace, patience, kindness, generosity, faithfulness, gentleness, and self-control. The Holy Spirit is the enlivening causality behind all these fruits. These fruits come forth in us and through us as a result of our having the Holy Spirit inside us, and yet they also feed our spirit at the same time.

The fruits of the Spirit are in two forms: fruits that are a blessing to us, and those that enable us to be a blessing to others. Love, joy, and peace are things we experience from inside us in our hearts and minds. These fruits then can (but don't necessarily need to) radiate to the outside and affect how we relate to others. To know and feel the love that God has for me is a wonderful mountain top experience. To be able to transmit to another person the intense inner feeling of being loved by God is impossible, but I can use my spiritual gifts of teaching or counseling or administration to bless your life in some outward way that will help you experience the grace of God.

Patience, kindness, generosity, faithfulness, gentleness and self-control are wonderful fruits of the Holy Spirit that show up in our behaviors towards others. Having these traits of patience, kindness, generosity, faithfulness, gentleness and self-control, are evidence that you genuinely have the other fruit of the spirit (love, peace and joy through the Holy Spirit) inside you as well.

Patience, kindness, generosity, faithfulness, gentleness and self-control, are the outward manifestations of the inward graces we receive through the Holy Spirit of love, peace and joy.

So how do we go about getting this palatial feast? Well the first this we need to remember is that the Lord prepares the table for us and God invites us to come in and eat. Jesus said, "I stand at the door and knock. If you hear my voice and open the door, I will come in, and we will share a meal together as friends." Jesus is bringing the spiritual food with him but just as God will not kick open the doors of our hearts God will not force us to sit and eat with Him. God operates within us by initiation, but even when invited God will not operate within us if our hearts and minds are not in the right place. That is why we must do the work I spoke about in the last two sermons of preparing the ground and pouring a foundation.

In moments of absolute crisis people are able to do miraculous feats of strength. For example, I have seen several credible accounts online of young men lifting up a car all by themselves to allow someone the car fell on to be extricated. In moments of absolute crisis in our lives we are capable of seeking God with amazing intensity, single minded focus, purity of heart, and openness that God is delighted to respond to. But in ordinary times and in times of lesser crisis, we cannot bring the same levels of focus, purity and intensity. So in ordinary time we need to do the work of preparing the ground, pouring the foundation and using the proper building materials.

God is like a strict parent who won't let His child come to the table until he has washed his hands, God will not let us come to feast at his table until we have washed our soul, by doing the work of clearing our conscience (taking a careful moral inventory), and creating a foundation of having the right attitude towards God which includes humility, desire to be pleasing to God, desire to know God by experience; the love of self, and our willingness to put our all into it. But God is also like the stereotype mother who always wants to feed her children until they are so stuffed that they can't move. God can feed us like that because unlike our physical bodies which are naturally limited in size and stop growing with age, our spiritual relationship can grow continually at any age and when massively fed grows massively.

So the bottom line take away from this chapter is that God has provided many ways for us to feed our spirit. There is an old saying you probably have heard, "You are what you eat." That is true spiritually as well, and is why it is a good idea for us to have a varied spiritual diet that includes: looking for God in action in the people and things around us, reading the Bible and other holy books, prayer, meditation, listening to music that touches our soul, using all the means of Grace and the fruit of the Spirit. All of these things build us up spiritually and sustain us for building our spiritual palace relationship with God.

I want to take a moment of prayer now to make sure our hearts and minds are in the right place with God for us to build up our relationship with God. Will you join me? Let us pray:

> Lord God, we You praise and give You thanks that in Your wisdom and love You call us to You. In Your grace and mercy, infinite patience and kindness You correct us as we are walking on Your path. Because we are walking on Your path You care for us, protect us and provide for us. You place a wall of spiritual protection around us, you give us signs along the way so that we don't get lost, and You give us spiritual nourishment to sustain us on the journey. Thank You God for loving so much that You grace us with so much and offer so much to us. Help us Father through the wonderful gift of Your Holy Spirit to live, love, believe and serve in ways that are acceptable to

You and that lead us always closer to You. In Jesus name we pray.

Questions for Self-Reflection

• Paul talked about our need to feed on real solid spiritual food. Where am I on the spectrum from being like a baby who needs milk and cannot eat solid food to being a mature adult who can eat the solid food of theology?

• What am I doing to feed myself spiritually?

• Do I read the Bible enough?

• Do I pray enough?

• Do I attend worship enough?

Scripture Quotes & Sermon Notes
Building Your Spiritual Palace – The Dining Room

Psalms 23:5 (NKJV) You prepare a table before me in the presence of my enemies; You anoint my head with oil; My cup runs over.

Psalms 23:5 (NLT) You prepare a feast for me in the presence of my enemies. You honor me by anointing my head with oil. My cup overflows with blessings.

Romans 8:15-16 (NRSV) [15]For you did not receive a spirit of slavery to fall back into fear, but you have received a spirit of adoption. When we cry, "Abba! Father!" [16]it is that very Spirit bearing witness with our spirit that we are children of God,

Galatians 5:22-23 (NRSV) [22]By contrast, the fruit of the Spirit is love, joy, peace, patience, kindness, generosity, faithfulness,

23gentleness, and self-control. There is no law against such things.

Matthew 4:3-4 (NRSV) 3The tempter came and said to him, "If you are the Son of God, command these stones to become loaves of bread." 4But he answered, "It is written, "One does not live by bread alone, but by every word that comes from the mouth of God.""

Hebrews 5:12-14 (NLT) [12]You have been believers so long now that you ought to be teaching others. Instead, you need someone to teach you again the basic things about God's word. You are like babies who need milk and cannot eat solid food. [13]For someone who lives on milk is still an infant and doesn't know how to do what is right. [14]Solid food is for those who are mature, who through training have the skill to recognize the difference between right and wrong.

John 6:47-51 (NLT) [47]"I tell you the truth, anyone who believes in me has eternal life. 48Yes, I am the bread of life! 49Your ancestors ate manna in the wilderness, but they all died. 50Anyone who eats the bread from heaven, however, will never die. 51I am the living bread that came down from heaven. Anyone who eats this bread will live forever; and this bread, which I will offer so the world may live, is my flesh."

1 Corinthians 10:16 (NLT) [16]When we bless the cup at the Lord's Table, aren't we sharing in the blood of Christ? And when we break the bread, aren't we sharing in the body of Christ?

1 Corinthians 11:27-29 (NLT) 27So anyone who eats this bread or drinks this cup of the Lord unworthily is guilty of sinning against the body and blood of the Lord. 28That is why you should examine yourself before eating the bread and drinking the cup. 29For if you eat the bread or drink the cup without honoring the body of Christ, you are eating and drinking God's judgment upon yourself.

Galatians 5:22-23 (NRSV) [22]By contrast, the fruit of the Spirit is love, joy, peace, patience, kindness, generosity, faithfulness, 23gentleness, and self-control. There is no law against such things.

1 Corinthians 10:1-4 (NLT) [1]I don't want you to forget, dear brothers and sisters, about our ancestors in the wilderness long ago. All of them were guided by a cloud that moved ahead of them, and all of them walked through the sea on dry ground… [3]All of them ate the same spiritual food, 4and all of them drank the same spiritual water. For they drank from the spiritual rock that traveled with them, and that rock was Christ.

We feed our spirit by looking for God in action in the people and things around us; reading the Bible and other holy books; prayer, meditation; listening to inspiring music; using all the means of Grace.

Chapter Ten: The Throne Room

Originally preached March 24, 2019

In the Old Testament the throne was literally the seat of the King's power and authority. It was the symbol of office. When God told David who was to succeed him as king he said of Solomon 'he is the one I will *place on your throne* (1 Kings 5:5)'. Solomon also had a throne room built in his palace which he called the Hall of Justice, where he sat to hear legal matters. The throne room is also the room where the king would receive important visitors.

In our spiritual palace throne room represents the place where we go to approach or be in the presence of God who is our authority. The expectation in the Bible – both testaments – is that we will seek to be in the presence of God. Psalm 42 has that wonderful quote: "My soul thirsts for God, for the living God. When shall I come and behold the face of God?" Psalm 63 says something similar, but adds the poetic imagery, "my soul thirsts for you; my flesh faints for you, as in a dry and weary land where there is no water."

There is also an expectation in both testaments that the truly good person will see the face of God, "For the righteous LORD loves justice. The virtuous will see his face." And, "Blessed are the pure in heart, for they shall see God." A spiritual palace relationship with God is one in which we are truly seeking to enter God's presence and are frequently successful in doing so. In this chapter I am using the *Throne Room* as a metaphor for how and where we approach and seek the face of God.

In this chapter about approaching God I will be focusing on a neglected aspect of approaching God that an excellent relationship with God (a spiritual palace) is incomplete without. I am speaking about a prayer life that includes and addresses all three persons of the Trinity. From my experience a Trinitarian approach to prayer is often neglected, both in sermons and in daily practice of most Christians: this was true for me, and it has proven to be true in many conversations with members of my churches over the years. How often do your prayers include speaking to all three persons of the godhead?

But before I get farther into that discussion, as always, let's take a moment to enter the subject with prayer:

> Lord God, You are God the Three in One, of one spiritual essence. In Your perfection and in Your love for us You desire that we seek You with all of our hearts, and that we seek not just a part of who You are but all of who you are. In three persons You are our Father and Creator, in Christ our brother and redeemer, and our sustainer through Your Spirit within us. You have made three ways for us to know You, three ways for us to relate to You; three ways to draw strength from You, and three ways to love You. Help us now and always to continually explore fullness of what it means to love You as Father, and Son and Holy Spirit. Amen.

Let us take a quick look at a story that illustrates the difficulty of talking about the Trinity. It takes place at Caesarea Philippi. Jesus asked the disciples, "Who do men say that I am?" His disciples answered, "Some say you are John the Baptist returned from the dead; others say you are Elijah, or another of the old prophets." And Jesus answered and said, "But who do you say that I am?" Peter answered and said, "You are the Logos, one person of the Trinity, being of one essence and nature with the father, and generated by but not created by the Father, being with the Father from the beginning, through whom the Father created, and who together with the Holy Spirit, is coequal with God, yet subordinate to God, three distinct persons and each member inseparable with and interpenetrating the other members."

Yes, that was a little trick I played on you: that last part is not scriptural; but it points out the difficulties theologians have had over the years to understand the mystery of the Trinity, of a God who is three in one. The exact relationship and interaction between the three parts of the Trinity is deep, and as we saw in my trick story, more than a little complicated. The Trinity is so deep and difficult to grasp that no less than six different heresies of the early church were related to the Trinity. So if you struggle to fully understand the exact nature and form of the relationship between the members of the Trinity you are in good company. To simplify things here is how I understand the Trinity: The Trinity is God in three persons; each person different in some ways but made one in that they share the same spiritual essence. Jesus explained it this way: "Whoever has seen me has seen the Father. How can you say, 'Show us the Father'...? Just believe that I am in the Father and the Father is in me" (John 14). How can Jesus have the Father in him, be in the Father and still be in the world? Because the Father is in him in a spiritual way, they share the same spiritual essence, which is also the substance of the Holy Spirit.

My second doctoral course at Asbury theological seminary was taught by Dr. Steve Seamons. Steve is exactly what I had pictured, hoped for and expected to find in my seminary instructors: a deeply humble, soft spoken, very intelligent man in his early 60s; a man of deep faith and an expert in his field. The class was *Doctor of Ministry 801: Theology of Ministry*. Dr. Seamons is an unabashed Trinitarian, which is to say that the theology he was teaching us was all about the Trinity. That was good with me because at that point, even after over twenty years as a pastor, the Trinity was a difficult subject for me.

Maybe you are smarted than I was, and maybe you are already on top of this subject but, up to that point in my life about 10 years ago, my prayers were generally always addressed to God our Father. I seldom prayed to Jesus, and I don't believe I ever prayed to the Holy Spirit, who I did not actually think of as a person. At that time, even though I had already been baptized by the Holy Spirit twice, I still thought about the Spirit as an impersonal force similar to electricity. What that class did for me was it helped me to realize both that the Spirit is a person of God, and very important: that each person of the Trinity is already in some level of relationship with me, therefore I need to work on my relationship with each person of the Trinity, not just with God the Father and/or Jesus, but also with the Holy Spirit.

In describing the actions of each person of the Trinity the Bible shows us three different ways that God relates to us: as our father and creator; as our savior, redeemer and brother, and as a sustaining, empowering and equipping Holy Spirit. The creator, redeemer and sustainer are three different persons, but they share the same spiritual essence which it what makes them one. The most important thing I learned from Dr. Seamons is that my prayer life is incomplete if it does not include all three persons of the Trinity. So now I begin my personal prayers by speaking to each person of the Trinity, and I begin every sermon with this short prayer:

> "I thank you God for the awesome privilege and responsibility of sharing Your word with Your people. May all that I say and all that we hear be acceptable in Your sight, for You are our creator, our redeemer, and our sustainer."

This is how I begin my personal daily prayer:

> Good morning Father; You are the eternal Creator, the maker of all things in the heavens and on the earth, the Lord God Almighty. You are my creator and my Father in heaven. Good morning Jesus, you are my

Lord and Savior; the Son of God and Son of Man, the gift of the Father's unfailing grace, the promise of my deliverance from sin and death. And I pray to You Holy Spirit, God present with us, in us, and around us. All love, praise, honor, glory, joy and thanks to You Father for Your love and power that are over all Your works, and for Your will that is always directed towards Your children's good. Thank You for allowing us to become Your children through our faith in You, in Jesus Christ, and through the indwelling of your Holy Spirit. You are the King of Creation and You are the one and only God.

God the Father sent the son and God revealed His nature to us through His son; and God lives with us and within us (by our invitation) through the Holy Spirit whom the Son prayed for and the Father sent. The Bible helps us to understand the relationship of the Trinity members to each other and shows us the different ways that we should relate to each member of the Trinity.

How we relate to each member of the Trinity is different. We relate to God as our creator, as the ultimate source of power and reality in the universe. We relate to God the father as St. Anselm called him, "the being than which nothing greater can be thought." In our prayer life we need to relate to God as our Father with all the humility and thankfulness we can muster, for our life and existence and the blessing so life we receive from Him each day. The apostle James tells us, "<u>Humble yourselves before the Lord</u>" and that is one of many passages that tell us humility is the correct way to approach our Father God. The humble approach to God is typified in the ACTS prayer; after the Lord's Prayer the ACTS prayer is probably the next best guide to how to relate to God. In the ACTS prayer we offer God, Adoration, Confession, Thanks, and all these things before we get to Supplication, or asking God for things.

Jesus, the son of God, was a man, a human being just as we are, but he the Son of God by virtue of being so entirely filled with the Holy Spirit as to be able to use the spiritual power of God to perform miracles, like walking on the water and raising the dead. So we relate to Jesus as our teacher, example, our brother, and as our Lord and Savior. Jesus said, "Whoever does the will of my Father in heaven is my brother and sister and mother" (Matt. 12:50). Being a brother is a friendship relationship; our spiritual palace needs to be pretty well under construction before we begin to truly feel that we are Jesus' brother or sister. In the meantime, we build up our relationship with Jesus by being thankful to Him every day because of what he suffered for us to take away our sins. Paul reminded us that by taking away our sins Jesus opened up the door for us to have this <u>new</u> and deeper type of <u>relationship</u> with God, where <u>God is not just our creator but our friend</u> (Romans 8:5-11). How wonderful it is to get to a place in your faith life where you can say, "Jesus is my brother, and I am a friend of God!"

Lastly, the way we relate to the Spirit. The apostle Paul tells us that our bodies are "temples of the Holy Spirit within us." According to Jesus God sent us the Holy Spirit to be both with us, as in around us, and to be in us: God's plan and desire is to fill us with Spirit (John 14:17), just as the apostles and disciples of Jesus were filled. According to Paul the Holy Spirit "joins with our spirit to affirm that we are God's children" (Romans 8:16 NLT). It is my experience that the Holy Spirit is the main way God relates to us: at times He comforts us, at times He fills us with joy and light, at times He terrifies us with His power, but in all things His role is to lead us closer to the Father.

Here are a few of the expressions of the fullness of God's love and grace that come to us through the Holy Spirit that we don't want to miss out on. As we have already heard, Paul tells us one work of the Spirit is to give us the fruits of the Spirit: peace, joy, love, strength, patience, kindness, and gentleness (Galatians 5:22-23). Another part of the work of the Spirit Paul describes this way: "God has sent the Spirit of his Son into our hearts, to prompt us to call out, "Abba, Father" (Galatians 4:6). In other words a work of the Spirit is to cause us to relate to God as our Father. Paul also says the Spirit calls us and prompts us to grow up in every way to Christ, who is the head" (Ephesians 4:15). The Spirit gives us each spiritual gifts, or as I understand them and experience them, God gives us supernatural assistance when we use our talents and abilities to serve God, so that the result of our service exceeds that which we could do on our own (1 Cor. 12:4, 11). Lastly Jesus said that God sends us the Spirit to comfort us, to be our advocate (John 14:16), and to help us find the right words when we need to defend our faith (Mark 13:11). The Holy Spirit is pretty busy!

We relate to the Spirit by praying for the Spirit. Jesus taught us to pray for the Holy Spirit; he said, "your heavenly Father [will] give the Holy Spirit to those who ask him" (Luke 11:13). We build up our relationship with the Holy Spirit by being open to having the Spirit to be inside us; by daily inviting the Holy Spirit to fill us; and by cleaning up the temple, i.e. preparing a place inside our heart where the Spirit can rest.

What I want to impress on you with this chapter is the idea that for too many of us we neglect the Holy Spirit in our prayer life and doing so cuts us off from experiencing the fullness of God's love and grace towards us. If you have already been spending time in your throne room praying to all three members of the Trinity then a) congratulations, and b) I hope this chapter has been at least a good reminder to you of what orthodox Christianity believes about the Trinity. But if up till now your prayer life has not included praying to all three members of the Holy Spirit then the throne room of your spiritual palace, the place you go to meet with God in prayer, will be missing a window or a wall until you do. I want to encourage you, from now on, to include at least a mention of all three members of the Trinity in your daily prayers.

One simple way to begin to include all three members of the Trinity in your prayer life is to begin your prayer by making what the Catholics refer to as 'the sign of the cross." You can make the sign of the cross physically by touching your right hand to your forehead, then to your stomach, then to your left then right shoulders (making the outline of a cross) and at the same time intoning "in the name of the Father (touch the forehead) and of the Son (stomach) and of the Holy Spirit (shoulders). Or you can, and I usually always do, make the sign of the cross mentally instead of physically.

I would like to invite you to join me in reciting a little prayer called the Gloria Patri as our closing for this chapter. "Glory be to the Father, and to the son, and to the Holy Ghost – as it was in the beginning, is now and ever shall be, world without amen."

Questions for Self-Reflection

- Have you ever prayed using the ACTS prayer?

- In your prayer life do you usually speak to all three persons of the Trinity?

- If not, why not?

- If not do you intend to from now on?

- If you are struggling to know the Holy Spirit as a person of the Trinity what steps can you take to change that situation?

Scripture Quotes
Building a Spiritual Palace: The Throne Room

1 Kings 5:5 (NLT) ⁵So I am planning to build a Temple to honor the name of the LORD my God, just as he had instructed my father, David. For the LORD told him, 'Your son, <u>whom I will place on your throne</u>, will build the Temple to honor my name.'

1 Kings 7:7 Solomon also <u>built the throne room, known as the Hall of Justice</u>, where he sat to hear legal matters. It was paneled with cedar from floor to ceiling.

Psalms 42:2 (NRSV) My soul thirsts for God, for the living God. When shall I come and behold the face of God?

Psalms 63:1 O God, you are my God, I seek you, my soul thirsts for you; my flesh faints for you, as in a dry and weary land where there is no water.

Psalms 11:7 (NLT) For the righteous LORD loves justice. The virtuous will see his face.

Matthew 5:8 (NKJV) Blessed are the pure in heart, for they shall see God.

John 14:8-9, 11, 15-17 (NRSV) 8Philip said to him, "Lord, show us the Father, and we will be satisfied." 9Jesus said to him, "Have I been with you all this time, Philip, and you still do not know me? <u>Whoever has seen me has seen the Father. How can you say, 'Show us the Father'...? Just believe that I am in the Father and the Father is in me</u>. Or at least believe because of the work you have seen me do... If you love me, obey my commandments. 16And <u>I will ask the Father, and he will give you another Advocate</u>, who will never leave you. 17He is <u>the Holy Spirit, who leads into all truth</u>. The world cannot receive him because it isn't looking for him and doesn't recognize him.

But <u>you know him because he lives with you now and later will be in you</u>.

James 4:10 (NLT) <u>Humble yourselves before the Lord</u>, and he will lift you up in honor.

Matthew 12:49-50 (NRSV) ⁴⁹And pointing to his disciples, he said, "Here are my mother and my brothers! ⁵⁰For <u>whoever does the will of my Father in heaven is my brother and sister and mother</u>."

Romans 5:8-11 (NLT) ⁸But God showed his great love for us by sending Christ to die for us while we were still sinners. ⁹And since we have been made right in God's sight by the blood of Christ, he will certainly save us from God's condemnation. ¹⁰For since <u>our friendship with God</u> was restored by the death of his Son while we were still his enemies, we will certainly be saved through the life of his Son. ¹¹So now we can rejoice in <u>our wonderful new relationship with God because our Lord Jesus Christ has made us friends of God</u>.

Galatians 5:22-23 But the Holy Spirit produces this kind of fruit in our lives: love, joy, peace, patience, kindness, goodness, faithfulness, 23gentleness, and self-control. There is no law against these things!

Galatians 4:6 And because we are his children, <u>God has sent the Spirit of his Son into our hearts, prompting us to call out,</u> "<u>Abba, Father</u>."

Ephesians 4:15 (TEV) Instead, by speaking the truth in a spirit of love, <u>we must grow up in every way to Christ</u>, who is the head.

Acts 4:31 (NRSV) ³¹When they had prayed, the place in which they were gathered together was shaken; and <u>they were all filled with the Holy Spirit</u> and spoke the word of God with boldness.

Romans 8:15-16 For you did not receive a spirit of slavery to fall back into fear, but you have received a spirit of adoption. When we cry, "Abba! Father!" [16]it is that very Spirit bearing witness with our spirit that we are children of God,

1 Corinthians 12:4-11 (NLT) [4]There are different kinds of spiritual gifts, but the same Spirit is the source of them all...A spiritual gift is given to each of us so we can help each other. [8]To one person the Spirit gives the ability to give wise advice; to another the same Spirit gives a message of special knowledge. [9]The same Spirit gives great faith to another, and to someone else the one Spirit gives the gift of healing. [10]He gives one person the power to perform miracles, and another the ability to prophesy. He gives someone else the ability to discern whether a message is from the Spirit of God or from another spirit. Still another person is given the ability to speak in unknown languages, while another is given the ability to interpret what is being said. [11]It is the one and only Spirit who distributes all these gifts. He alone decides which gift each person should have.

Mark 13:11 (TEV) [11]And when you are arrested and taken to court, do not worry ahead of time about what you are going to say; when the time comes, say whatever is then given to you. For the words you speak will not be yours; they will come from the Holy Spirit.

1 Corinthians 6:19 (NRSV) [19]Or do you not know that <u>your body is a temple of the Holy Spirit</u> <u>within you,</u> which you have from God, and that you are not your own?

Luke 11:13 (NLT) 13So if your sinful people know how to give good gifts to your children, how much more will <u>your heavenly Father give the Holy Spirit to those who ask him.</u>"

Romans 8:16 For his Spirit <u>joins with our spirit</u> to affirm that we are God's children.

Chapter Eleven: The Living Room

Originally Preached April 28, 2019

This chapter is titled *The Living Room* a living room is the place you hang out with and socialize with family and friends; and I am going to talk about the spiritual practices of koinonea which many churches and Christians associate with hanging out with or fellowshipping with other Christians. Koinonea is a Greek word that is usually translated in our Bibles as Fellowship. When you hear the word fellowship what do you think about? Until recently I thought about the "Fellowship Halls" that most Methodist churches seem to have; and I thought of Christian fellowship as meaning hanging out with and socializing with our fellow Christians with everybody being on their best behavior. But as I researched Biblical koinonea I discovered that while it includes socializing it is far more than that; the Bible speaks about koinonea in five ways, each of which can be applied as a spiritual practice by the believer who is seeking to build up their relationship with God. In the book of the Acts of the Apostles, we are told that after Pentecost, the believers devoted themselves to the apostles' teaching, and to fellowship [koinonea], to sharing in meals, taking communion, and to prayer. Since the founders of the Christian church saw koinonea as an essential part of the practice of Christianity that is something we ought to be instructed by.

But before I get farther into the subject would you join me in a prayer?

> Lord God, you are calling all of us into koinonea with You and with each other. Help us Lord to grow continually in our knowledge and awareness of all the ways that koinonea can be expressed as a part of a growing relationship with You.

In my appointment at St. Andrew's UMC in Brandon as Associate Pastor I was put in charge of evangelism, and koinonea. St. Andrews was organized for ministry using the ministry plan outlined by Rick Warren in his best-selling book, "The Purpose Driven Church." Warren calls for churches to organize around five ministry areas – discipleship, worship, missions, evangelism, and koinonea. At that time I was a little sarcastic about it and I used to say to myself, "Why say fellowship when you can say koinonea?" Calling it the Koinonea ministry instead of fellowship seemed pretentious to me; I mean there are Greek words for discipleship, missions, evangelism and worship, but we didn't use the Greek words for them, just Koinonea.

It wasn't until many years later that I found out I was wrong: there was a good reason not to translate the Greek word koinonea to fellowship because koinonea takes in much more than just fellowship. Since the New Testament was originally written in Greek, and all modern versions of the Bible are translations from the Greek, when you want to know the most accurate translation of a word it is good to look at the Greek version and see how others have translated it. In Strong's Exhaustive Concordance of the Bible the Greek word koinonea is defined in five ways: **socializing, communication, partnership, sharing in ministry, and unity**. These five components of koinonea can be useful as spiritual practices to help expand our spiritual palace (ad some new dimensions to our discipleship efforts). While many of the things that we need to do to build up our relationship with God can be done by ourselves, such as examining our conscience, or reading the Bible, or praying, koinonea is entirely about things that we do with other people.

The Harvard Medical School published an article in 2015 entitled, "Strengthen relationships for longer, healthier life" that said:

> Social relationships not only give us pleasure, they also influence our long-term health in ways every bit as powerful as adequate sleep, a good diet, and not smoking. Dozens of studies have shown that people who have satisfying relationships with family,

friends, and their community are happier, have fewer health problems, and live longer.

The article also pointed out that a lack of social relationships is associated with poor health, with depression and later-life cognitive decline. One study they mentioned examined data from more than 309,000 people and found that lack of strong relationships increased the risk of premature death from all causes by 50% — an effect on mortality risk that is as bad for you as smoking up to 15 cigarettes a day. In Romans Paul writes: "I am planning to go to Spain, and when I do, I will stop off in Rome. And after I have enjoyed your fellowship [koinonea] for a little while, you can provide for my journey" (15:24 NLT). This is koinonea fellowship is purely in the form of socialization, hanging out with likeminded friends, and we have seen that socialization is important for your physical health, and good physical health eliminates the barrier that bad physical health sometimes is to good spiritual health.

Christian fellowship or Koinonea has all the health benefits of non-religious relationships but also has additional benefits, spiritually and emotionally. In the Methodist tradition, John Wesley, the founder of Methodism stressed the importance of what he called the Means of Grace, which he described as the six most easily accessible ways God has provided to us to enable us to experience God's grace. Wesley's six primary means of grace are reading the Bible, prayer, fasting, acts of charity, taking the sacraments, and Christian conversation.

Christian conversation is a part of the Biblical understanding of koinonea. Paul writes in his letter to Philemon, "My prayer is that our fellowship [koinonea] with you as believers will bring about a deeper understanding of every blessing we have in our life in union with Christ." That is the way Christian communication is supposed to work; it refreshes us and helps Christians come to a deeper understanding of the blessings of relationship with God through Jesus Christ. The book of

Proverbs put it this way, "As iron sharpens iron, so a friend sharpens a friend." You can participate in Christian conversation through attending a Sunday school, or a Bible study group, or any time you purposely seek out another believer for the purpose of talking about something related to your faith or theirs.

In Paul's first letter to the Corinthians Paul writes: "God is faithful; by him you were called into the fellowship [koinonea] of his Son, Jesus Christ our Lord." In this verse Paul is using koinonea meaning partnership in the organization – we are called into [koinonea] partnership with Jesus. In fact, the New Living Translation doesn't even use the word fellowship when it translates koinonea in this verse; it says God "has invited you into partnership with his Son, Jesus Christ our Lord." In Acts 2:47 we read "each day the Lord added to their fellowship [koinonea] those who were being saved." So koinonea in these passages is used to mean we are called or invited into partnership in the organization or church of Jesus Christ.

In Paul's second letter to the Corinthians (8:4) Paul talks about the fellowship [koinonea] of ministering to believers. So our partnership koinonea with Christ expresses itself in our participation in His ministry. Here is what Paul wrote: "They begged us again and again for the privilege of sharing in the gift and the fellowship [koinonea] of the ministering to the believers in Jerusalem." So in this passage koinonea is clearly used to mean sharing in ministry.

The last spiritual discipline of koinonea I want to specially lift up is koinonea expressed as unity with God. In his first letter John writes: "We proclaim to you what we ourselves have actually seen and heard so that you may have fellowship [koinonea] with us. And our fellowship [koinonea] is with the Father and with his Son, Jesus Christ." In this passage koinonea or fellowship is seen as a unity with God or as an intimate closeness with God. John tells us that the way to increase our unity with God is simply to obey God's commandments to love God and to love others. So unity with God koinonea comes from practicing our love for God and others.

Well thus far in this chapter we have seen that koinonea, which our Bible generally translates as *fellowship*, includes socialization, Christian communication, partnership with Christ, sharing in the ministry of Christ, and unity with or intimate closeness with Christ. Did you know all of that was included in "fellowship"? So fellowship in our Bible is more than just having fun together; there is a deeper purpose behind our church picnics, and our covered dish suppers, our volleyball games, our exchanging the peace and our coffee hour fellowship times. These activities are supposed to help us enjoy each other's company; they are supposed to help us feel more comfortable with each other so that we are more willing to engage in meaningful Christian conversation with each other. Our fellowship is supposed to strengthen our partnership with Christ, and to facilitate or make it more likely that we will join together and participate more fully in the ministry of Jesus Christ. And all these things together are spiritual disciplines that are good for our physical, mental and emotional health and at the same time bring us into closer unity with God through Christ.

We who are seeking to grow as disciples can use the definition of koinonea as a checklist for our spiritual progress: do I socialize with other Christians? Do I engage in Christian conversation for the good of my soul and theirs? Am I in partnership with Christ – and participating in his ministry? Do I love God and others in such a way that I feel unity with God through Christ? And if I am lacking in any of these areas what do I need to do to improve?

For many of us, the Easter and Christmas holidays mean family gatherings, getting together with friends, and maybe even participating with them in some of the special religious activities that church offers like attending a cantata, or a church dinner, or a special worship service. These occasions are an opportunity to practice koinonea with the ones we love most and / or are already in close relationship with, to exchange ideas and thoughts about God and Christian living, and perhaps lend a supportive ear or shoulder. But any time is a good time to strengthen your social relationship ties with others. Here are two ways to strengthen your social relationship ties. First is to start with those relationships you already have that are most meaningful to you. Find an activity or activities you can do together that are most likely to bring joy to both you and the people you care about. Second is make sure to make time for this: it is so easy to want to do this and often we don't make time so delegate or discard tasks that eat into your relationship time, or do those tasks together with family or friends as a way to turn your chores into relationship times.

At the very least we can remember that when we join together at coffee hour, and when we greet each other and exchange the peace on Sunday mornings, our fellowship times have a higher purpose. Would you join me in a prayer?

> Lord, my prayer is that my fellowship with other believers will bring about a deeper understanding me of every blessing which You offer us in union with Christ. Help me remember Lord, that You are inviting me to so much by inviting me to koinonea with You. May I be found faithful in koinonea with You and every good thing You are calling me to. Thank you, Lord, I pray this in Jesus name.

Questions for Self-Reflection

• Do I make a point of making time for socializing with other Christians?

• Do I regularly engage in Christian Communication?

- Am I doing an adequate job of sharing in the ministry and mission of Christ?

- Do I feel a unity with God the Father through Christ?

Chapter 11: The Living Room
Scripture Quotes

Philemon 1:6 (TEV) My prayer is that our fellowship with you as believers will bring about a deeper understanding of every blessing which we have in our life in union with Christ.

Proverbs 27:17 (NLT) As iron sharpens iron, so a friend sharpens a friend.

Acts 2:42 (NLT) All the believers devoted themselves to the apostles' teaching, and to fellowship, and to sharing in meals (including the Lord's Supper), and to prayer.

1 Corinthians 1:9 (NRSV) God is faithful; by him you were called into the fellowship of his Son, Jesus Christ our Lord.10I appeal to you, dear brothers and sisters, by the authority of our Lord Jesus Christ, to live in harmony with each other. Let there be no divisions in the church. Rather, be of one mind, united in thought and purpose…24But to those called by God to salvation, both Jews and Gentiles, Christ is the power of God and the wisdom of God…30God has united you with Christ Jesus. For our benefit God made him to be wisdom itself. Christ made us right with God; he made us pure and holy, and he freed us from sin.

1 Corinthians 1:9 (NLT) God will do this, for he is faithful to do what he says, and he has invited you into partnership with his Son, Jesus Christ our Lord.

2 Corinthians 8:4 They begged us again and again for the privilege of sharing in the gift and the fellowship [koinonea] of the ministering to the believers in Jerusalem.

1 John 1:3-4 We proclaim to you what we ourselves have actually seen and heard so that you may have fellowship with us. And our fellowship is with the Father and with his Son, Jesus Christ. 4We are writing these things so that you may fully share our joy.

Strengthen relationships for longer, healthier life. Harvard Health Publishing, The Harvard Medical School. www.health.harvard.edu.

Chapter Twelve: The Bedroom

Originally Preached May 19, 2019

No palace would be complete without a bedroom. Your bedroom is a very important room in your spiritual palace relationship with God because, among other reasons, in an average lifespan you will spend more time in that room than in any other room or place. About 25 years of your life will be spent in that one room, so if you can make that room a place that helps you to serve or grow in your relationship with God you will be redeeming some of that time, and helping yourself to grow spiritually. One of the younger members of my congregation, told me after church on the day I preached the sermon this chapter was based on, "When I heard what you were preaching on, I said to my father, 'This is going to be weird. But it wasn't, it was really good." I mention that in case you the reader have similar apprehensions.

Will you join me in a prayer?

> Lord God, You gave life and form to us and to every living thing on this planet. You are intimately aware of our desires and impulses. In Your love for us Your will and plan is that we treat every gift You give us with respect and appreciation. Guide us in what is written and what is read that it might serve us making us grow in our understanding of the love that You have for us and in our respect and appreciation for our sexuality and every other gift You give us? Thank You Father.

If you are already picturing in your mind what the master bedroom for your spiritual palace looks like, well let me say we are going in a different direction - the bedroom is a metaphor for marriage and sexuality. This chapter is about Christian marriage in particular and sexuality as God wants us to practice it because these things can either be a help or a hindrance to one's spiritual development.

Considering how important the issues related to sex and sexuality are in human relationships it is not surprising that the Bible has relatively much to say about it. The Old Testament, particularly in the first five books of the Bible, gives detailed list of the various prohibited behaviors, and assigns punishments for each. The New Testament does not go into the same level of specificity, but the Apostle Paul addresses a number of issues related to human sexuality and marriage in several letters, and especially in his First Letter to the Corinthians.

When Paul was writing his first letter the church in Corinth had only been in existence for a few years, Paul having established it a few years before on his first missionary journey. The church was dealing with questions and problems about Christian life and faith that and they had written to Paul for advice, and first Corinthians was written in response to their letter. Corinth at that time was a large, beautiful, wealthy Greek city on the shores of the Mediterranean Sea. Corinth was the capital of the Roman government in that area of Greece. Today, 2000 years later some of the majestic stone structures from Paul's day are still partially standing and they show how wealthy that town was. Paul wrote to them to both inspire them in faith and to speak to the issues that were dividing the church, including questions about human sexuality and marriage.

Paul wrote, "Now, getting down to the questions you asked in your letter to me. First, is it a good thing to have sexual relations?" Why would they ask a question like that? Because a number of the church members believed that the return of Christ and the end of the world was so close at hand that it was better to not marry, to remain celibate and just concentrate your attention on your relationship with God. So they ask Paul, "Is it a good thing to have sexual relations?" And his answer was,

"Certainly— but only within a certain context. It's good for a man to have a wife, and for a woman to have a husband. Sexual drives are strong, but marriage is strong enough to contain them and provide for a balanced and fulfilling sexual life in a world of sexual disorder…" Paul's answer to them is that God's plan for our sexuality is that it is best limited to and expressed in a marital relationship; and 2000 years later that is still true.

Later he adds this piece of advice for those who are already married: "And don't be wishing you were someplace else or with someone else. Where you are right now is God's place for you. Live and obey and love and believe right there. God, not your marital status, defines your life." This advice of Paul's goes together with the 10th commandment, which says do not covet, and it also goes with what Jesus said about marriage. Jesus basically said that marriage is a sacred bond that we enter into with the help and blessing of God, it is intended to be mutually exclusive, with the two partners becoming bonded as one person in an emotional and spiritual way. Jesus said,

> "Haven't you read the scripture that says that in the beginning the Creator made people male and female? [5] And God said, 'For this reason a man will leave his father and mother and unite with his wife, and the two shall become one flesh'? [6]So they are no longer two, but one flesh. Therefore what God has joined together, let no one separate."

What I get from this teaching of Jesus, is also what I have found in my experience as a pastor and in my relationship with my wife Anna: that as a rule you don't find your soul mate and then get married, you get married and become soul mates over time as you practice Christian love for each other.

I mentioned in Chapter Seven that the Greeks have three words for love; three words which our Bible translators all translate into English as love: *eros* which is romantic love; *philia* which is brotherly love, the kind of love you have for a close friend or sibling; and *agape* or Christian love. Paul writes about agape or Christian love in the 13th chapter of 1st Corinthians, "Love [agape] is patient and kind; it is not jealous or conceited or proud; love [agape] is not ill-mannered or selfish or irritable; love [agape] does not keep a record of wrongs; love [agape] is not happy with evil, but is happy with the truth. Love [agape] never gives up; and its faith, hope, and patience never fail." That kind of love is different from romantic love – and when you practice Christian love in your romantic relationship your romantic love gets better, because agape love inside you makes you a more considerate, forgiving and patient person and those are great things to have in a romantic relationship.

All Christians are called to practice agape love, and you don't have to be married or in a romantic relationship to practice Christian love. Agape love can be directed towards anyone precisely because it is not romantic love; it is loving others in the way that God loves us. When you practice being loving towards others with agape love, it helps you become more filled with love in general and love for God and being filled with love also naturally makes you much more appreciative about just being alive and all of that makes you a happier and more joy-filled person. Adding philia or brotherly love to a romantic relationship also strengthens it by adding another layer or dimension to the relationship.

The author of the book of Proverbs has a lot to say about marriage, both the good and the bad; about the good he says, "a good wife is a gift from the Lord." You can also read it the other way too, "a good husband is a gift from the Lord;" that is the good marriage. About the bad he writes, "It's better to live alone in the corner of an attic than with a quarrelsome wife in a lovely home" or we could say with a quarrelsome spouse." A happy marriage is a foretaste of the joys of heaven; an unhappy marriage can be a foretaste of hell. In Ecclesiastes we read that

God intends marriage to be a blessing to us, "Enjoy life with the wife whom you love, all the days of your vain life that are given you under the sun, because that is your portion in life and in your toil at which you toil under the sun." So the message the Bible is sharing in these passages is that human sexuality, expressed within a happy marriage, is a part of God's plan to bless our lives.

In the Ten Commandments the seventh commandment is, "You shall not commit adultery" (Exodus 20:14). The Old Testament is death on adultery; literally: in both Leviticus and Deuteronomy we read the same law: "If a man is discovered committing adultery, both he and the woman must die." Did you know the Bible has the death penalty for adultery? How many people do you know who would have been put to death if that law was still in effect? The reason the Bible has the death penalty for adultery is God is trying to make it clear to us that marriage is a sacred vow we take that we need to honor, and we must take it very seriously. Here is what Paul has to say about this subject: "Run from sexual sin! No other sin so clearly affects the body as this one does. For sexual immorality is a sin against your own body." The book of Proverbs also spends a lot of time warning us to stay away from adultery and admonishing us to remain faithful to our marriage vows.

One of the great challenges of the human condition is that sins related to sexuality start out as normal, healthy impulses or desires that we take to unhealthy extremes. For example, envy starts out as admiration; when it becomes compulsive and all-consuming it is a sin. Lust starts out as natural normal healthy attraction; when it becomes compulsive and all-consuming it is a sin. And it is not just sexually related sins, it is natural and normal to get angry, but anger we hold onto becomes poisonous hatred. It is normal to enjoy food, but to an extreme it leads to unhealthiness. It is normal to enjoy resting but taken too far it becomes sloth or self-destructive laziness. God sets things as sins because he loves us and wants what is best for us

- what is healthiest for us emotionally, spiritually and physically. As a rule what God deems as good is also good for us mentally, emotionally, physically and spiritually; and what God deems as bad is bad for us mentally, emotionally, physically and spiritually.

The Bible has a lot more to say about sex and human sexuality, I have only skimmed over the surface here; but I have read everything the Bible says about sex and human sexuality many times and I can give you a summary: basically the totality of what the Bible says about human sexuality it is that human sexuality is a powerful force. It is intended by God to bless us, and God's plan for our greatest blessing is that it be expressed in a monogamous (not monotonous) marital relationship. A monogamous marriage, in which both partners express love for each other with romantic, brotherly and Christian love will give us great satisfaction and be the healthiest for us.

Now there are three other things I want to mention about the bedroom: the first is about clothing. The bedroom closet is where most of us keep most of our clothing. Paul tells us when it comes to clothing, he wants us to be content with what we have and not to spend a lot on our clothing or be overly concerned with our appearance. Jesus said we should not focus on or worry about our clothing; but instead we should be seeking the Kingdom of God and righteousness (Matthew 6:25-33). Basically, what God wants us to remember about clothing is: what is most important is our relationship with God and not what we are wearing.

Our bedroom is also where we do most of our resting and sleeping. Getting a good night's rest is very important to our physical health, a healthy adult should get at least 6 hours of sleep a night, and now the experts say on average you should get no more than 8 hours. Getting the right amount of rest is wonderful for your health; it helps keep our weight and blood pressure down; and sleeping allows our bodies to heal and renew our strength. Emotionally, a good night's sleep is a break from whatever is troubling you. How many times have you been upset, and someone tells you to sleep on it, and you go to sleep and wake up feeling better? A good night's sleep helps you to heal emotionally. Mentally a good night's sleep helps you to be clearer headed – better able to think. Spiritually, if the rest of you is suffering emotionally, mentally, or physically your spirituality will suffer as well, so resting well is important for your spirituality. God is so concerned that we take time to rest regularly that the third of the ten commandments is to take a day of complete rest each week (Exodus 20:8-11).

Lastly, your bedroom should be a place of prayer. Some of the most important and intense prayer times of my life have happened while I was praying on my bed. When we make our bedroom also our prayer room, we do a good thing for ourselves spiritually. I try to begin each morning with God and end each day with God; even it is a quick "thank you God for this day!" The first thing I say when I wake up is, "Good morning God, thank You for this day." And the last thing I say when my head hits the pillow is "Thank You for this day" In this way you can bracket your whole day with prayer. Jesus said, "When you pray, go into your room (he is talking here about your bedroom), and shut the door and pray to your father in private." Praying the Lord's Prayer together in church is one of my favorite things. -It feels so good to know we are all sharing together in prayer, praying the same thing together. But praying alone in quiet is both more personal and more intense, and we should definitely do both.

I have found that for me, my main prayer time needs to be in the morning. I found that lying on my bed praying at the end of a long day tends to put me to sleep long before I have finished saying all I want to say. That is a nice way to go to sleep, but it is frustrating when you have prayers that you want to say but fall asleep before you say them. Everybody is different and it may not be that way for you, but if you do find that you fall asleep while you are praying, then I would suggest that you use a shorter prayer like the Lord's prayer at night and make your main prayer time in the morning or day time.

So what I would like you to take with you from this chapter is that with a little thought and effort you can make your bedroom a place that helps you build up your spiritual palace relationship with God.

Scripture Quotes
Chapter 11: The Bedroom

1 Corinthians 7:1-4 (TMSG) 1Now, getting down to the questions you asked in your letter to me. First, <u>is it a good thing to have sexual relations</u>? 2Certainly—but only within a certain context. It's good for a man to have a wife, and for a woman to have a husband. Sexual drives are strong, but marriage is strong enough to contain them and provide for a balanced and fulfilling sexual life in a world of sexual disorder. 3The marriage bed must be a place of mutuality—the husband seeking to satisfy his wife, the wife seeking to satisfy her husband. 4Marriage is not a place to "stand up for your rights." Marriage is a decision to serve the other, whether in bed or out.

1 Corinthians 7:17 (TMSG) 17And <u>don't be wishing you were someplace else or with someone else. Where you are right now is God's place for you. Live and obey and love and believe right there</u>. God, not your marital status, defines your life. Don't think I'm being harder on you than on the others. I give this same counsel in all the churches.

Matthew 19:4-6 (NRSV) 4He answered, "Have you not read that the one who made them at the beginning 'made them male and female,' 5and said, 'For this reason a man shall leave his father and mother and be joined to his wife, and the two shall become one flesh'? 6So <u>they are no longer two, but one flesh</u>. Therefore what God has joined together, let no one separate."

1 Corinthians 13:4-7 (TEV) 4Love is patient and kind; it is not jealous or conceited or proud; 5love is not ill-mannered or selfish or irritable; love does not keep a record of wrongs; 6love is not happy with evil but is happy with the truth. 7Love never gives up; and its faith, hope, and patience never fail.

Proverbs 19:14 (CEV) You may inherit all you own from your parents, but <u>a sensible wife is a gift from the Lord</u>.

Proverbs 21:9 (NLT) It's better to live alone in the corner of an attic than with a quarrelsome wife in a lovely home.

Ecclesiastes 9:9 (NRSV) 9Enjoy life with the wife whom you love, all the days of your vain life that are given you under the sun, because that is your portion in life and in your toil at which you toil under the sun.

Deuteronomy 22:22 (NLT) [22]"If a man is discovered committing adultery, both he and the woman must die. In this way, you will purge Israel of such evil.

1 Corinthians 6:18 Run from sexual sin! No other sin so clearly affects the body as this one does. For sexual immorality is a sin against your own body.

Matthew 6:25-33 "That is why I tell you not to worry about everyday life—whether you have enough food and drink, or enough clothes to wear. ... 33Seek the Kingdom of God above all else, and live righteously, and he will give you everything you need.

1 Timothy 6:6-8 Yet true godliness with contentment is itself great wealth. 7After all, we brought nothing with us when we came into the world, and we can't take anything with us when we leave it. 8So if we have enough food and clothing, let us be content.

Matthew 6:6 But when you pray, go into your room and shut the door behind you, and pray to your Father in private. Then your Father, who sees everything, will reward you.

Chapter Thirteen: The Kitchen

Originally preached May 26, 2019

In this chapter entitled *The Kitchen*, kitchen is a metaphor for using eating as an opportunity for spiritual growth. How great it is that we can take eating - something every one of us does at least daily and use it as a tool to help us grow spiritually! In this chapter I am going to talk about three ways that you can use food to help you grow spiritually, and each one has the potential to deeply influence your spirituality and help us build our spiritual palace relationship with God.

I want to start this chapter with a funny observation I read as I was researching for this chapter about food. Did you know that the Japanese eat very little fat compared to Americans and British people, and yet they suffer fewer heart attacks than Americans and British people? Oddly, both the French and the Italians eat a lot fatter, in cheese and olive oil, than Americans and British people, and they drink large amounts of red wine, but they also suffer fewer heart attacks than Americans and British people do. What is the conclusion? We don't need to worry what we eat and drink: it's speaking English that bad for your heart.

Would you join me in prayer?

> Lord God, Eternal Creator, I want to be filled with love and joy and peace through Your Holy Spirit inside me. Jesus, you taught us that those of us who listen to Your teachings and obey them are like those who build their house on a solid rock. I want that relationship with You God, and even more than a house I want a spiritual palace relationship with You as my Father, in Christ my redeemer, and in Your Holy Spirit my sustainer. I want the kind of relationship with You God

where I can truthfully say with the writer of the 23rd psalm *the Lord is my shepherd* – He will watch over me and protect me. *My cup runneth over* - I am filled to overflowing with Your love and joy and peace, and I know that I will live in Your house forever. So open my mind to Your leading and inspiration and my heart to Your love and power? In Jesus name I ask all these things. Thank You Lord. Amen.

In the first chapter of the Bible, in Genesis, before God rested at the end of the sixth day, he gave human beings food (1:29). In the last chapter of the Bible in Revelation (22:14) eating is also mentioned. From the first chapter to the last chapter, food is prominently mentioned throughout the Bible as both a necessity and as a God given pleasure. At the time the Bible was written food was a lot more difficult to obtain and to preserve and there were fewer choices of items than we enjoy today. It is a safe bet that food was not taken for granted in Jesus' day in the way that it is by so many of us today. Perhaps it is because food is so available to modern time Christians that we tend to overlook the spiritual aspects of eating.

In the Old Testament the book of Ecclesiastes (3:13, 5:18, 8:15, & 9:7) really emphasizes that food is to be seen as a reward from God for our labors. In the New Testament the most prominent message about food is given in Jesus' Sermon on the Mount in which he basically says that we need to have the right attitude about food:

> "This is why I tell you: do not be worried about the food and drink you need in order to stay alive, or about clothes for your body. After all, isn't life worth more than food? And isn't the body worth more than clothes?" (Matthew 6:25-34 TEV).

There is an old saying, *some people eat to live, and others live to eat.* The Bible wants us to know that eating like everything else in our lives is to be viewed in light of our relationship with God. The right attitude is to stay mentally at the balance point between appreciating it and obsessing about it.

In Jesus' prayer, the Lord's Prayer, the second thing he taught us in it is to ask for is this day's daily bread, but only after we first praised God and prayed for the Kingdom of God to come to earth. Then we are to ask only for *this day's daily bread.* He didn't teach us to ask for a feast, or to ask for tomorrow's bread. Paul writes, in his first letter to Timothy: "if we have food and clothing, we will be content with these." The lesson to us from all of this is that we are to ask for what we need today, and we should be content if we have enough. We take life one day at a time and don't worry or obsess about the future. This is what Jesus said about food:

> "Look at the birds. They don't plant or harvest or store food in barns, for your heavenly Father feeds them. And aren't you far more valuable to him than they are?... Seek the Kingdom of God above all else, and live righteously, and he will give you everything you need." (Matthew 5:26, 33, NLT)

By telling us not to ask for more than we need, and by teaching us not to obsess about food, Jesus was indirectly indicating that our attitude about food affects our spirituality. The right attitude towards food can help us build up our relationship with God, and the wrong attitude can move us away from God. The wrong attitude is to be out of balance in your attitude: either to idolize food and make it more important in your life than God is, or to take it for granted and not be grateful for the amazing and miraculous gift that food is; from its production to its consumption and use in our bodies.

In the opening paragraph of this chapter I said there are three ways we can use food to help us grow closer to God, two of which can be used every day. The first and most obvious way to use food for spiritual growth is to begin every meal with a prayer: this is using food to bring your attention to God. I like to use the Lord's Prayer when I am eating alone and at our family meal times, for several reasons. First, it is the prayer Jesus taught us, and I am humble enough to realize that Jesus created a much more perfect prayer than I can. Second, I am convinced that every Christian should pray the Lord's Prayer daily and linking it to food can establish a routine to ensure that you pray the Lord's Prayer daily. Lastly, praying the Lord's Prayer in a family meal gets everybody at the table involved in the prayer, and I think that is a great thing to do (besides they also know I can't pray as well as Jesus can). In all seriousness, if you pray even a very short prayer before every meal, even like, "Thanks God!" that one behavior alone (something everybody can and should do every day out of respect for God) will deepen your relationship with God and change your life.

The second thing we can do to go a little deeper in using food to build our relationship with God is to eat "mindfully." Mindfully means that you bring all your attention to what and how you are eating. Christian Author Lisa Kelly wrote: "In a spirituality that seeks to find God in all things, finding God in taste is the most overlooked experience and yet easily the most accessible." I think she completely nailed it: taste and food is one of the most overlooked ways to appreciate God. Have you ever eaten something that tasted so good or had such a great meal that you just said, "Wow, thank you God!"? I know I have. But it doesn't have to be a feast for us to bring our attention to what we are eating and to enjoy it and be thankful to God for it.

A member of my church took me out to lunch at an Italian Restaurant, and after lunch he and I were speaking with the waitress and with the owner who is the chef. We got on the subject of cell phones. The waitress said she hates them because it is hard to get young people to stop playing with their phones and look at the menu and then to lower them again long enough to give her their order. The owner said he thought cell phones were both good and bad, the good is now when it takes the usual 20 minutes to make and cook a pizza they don't stare at him in frustration that it is taking so long because everyone is playing with their phone the whole time. But the bad thing, they both agreed, was seeing all the people sitting at tables during dinner and no one is paying attention to either their food or to the other people at the table; they are on their phones the whole time.

Everybody sitting at the table with their cell phone in their hand is a perfect example of distracted eating. These days, time is our most precious commodity, and most of us, I know I am guilty of this; we don't pay much attention to our food while to eating. There is an old story that Albert Einstein was stopped by a reporter for a brief interview as he was walking across the Princeton campus. After the interview he asked the reporter, "When you stopped me, which way was I going?" The reporter pointed and said, "That way." Einstein said, "Oh good then I've had lunch already." Einstein at least had a good excuse – he was figuring out the whole universe. I know that I sometimes am in such a hurry or so distracted that an hour after I eat I have to think about it for a few seconds to remember if I ate, let alone what or even how it tasted,much less to the miracles involved in its production.

The Bible affirms that a good meal is a gift from God, but you don't have to be a Christian to appreciate the miracle that food is: a Zen Buddhist Monk, Thich Nhat Hanh, wrote: "If you truly get in touch with a piece of carrot, you get in touch with the soil, the rain, the sunshine. You get in touch with Mother Earth and eating in such a way, you feel in touch with true life, your roots, and that is meditation. If we chew every morsel of our food in that way, we become grateful and when you are grateful, you are happy." Eating mindfully is bringing your attention to what you are eating with thankfulness, which turns eating into a spiritual blessing.

So saying a prayer of thanks before every meal, and mindfulness when we eat are two things that we can do daily that will help bring us closer to God. The third way to use food to build your relationship with God is to turn eating into a true spiritual exercise. The famous 16th century mystic St. Ignatius of Loyola created a spiritual exercise called *Rules for Eating While on A Spiritual Retreat*. His spiritual exercise is really just an expanded form of mindfulness. I have modified Ignatius' exercise and have used it several times both on retreat, at home, and in my office and have really enjoyed it and benefited spiritually from it.

A SPIRITUAL EXERCISE USING FOOD

This is an exercise you need to do where you can be by yourself because it requires us not to be distracted by people or things so we can concentrate entirely on the meal (by the way I have a summary of the steps of this exercise at the end of this chapter). It is best to use a cold meal such as a sandwich and chips and a piece of fruit or salad and a drink, so that you will not focus on the fact that your food is getting cold. The spiritual exercise begins with taking about ten minutes to center our mind in the exercise. Of course we want to begin with a prayer such as this one.

> Lord God please be present with me in this exercise and help me to have my heart and mind open to Your leading and inspiration through Your Spirit so that I may get the most possible benefit from it. Thank you, God, for this food and the work of so many that made it all possible for me today.

Centering our mind in the exercise consists of thinking about the miracle of the food itself and all that went into it being in front of us. If someone were to point out to us or remind us to think about it, we can immediately start thinking about what a bunch of miracles and blessings are involved in our morning bowl of frosted flakes. Just the creation itself is miraculous: how amazing is it that God created the universe in such a way that our planet formed at just the right distance from the sun to allow for life, and that it rotates at just the right speed and angle of rotation to allow for the maximum areas to grow plants, with just the right materials to make growing plants the easiest. We can think about the interaction between the sun's energy and the atmosphere's air and water and the dirt that all together allow a small seed to grow into a plant we can eat and that creates more seeds for future plants? And the DNA in each plant cell that guides its formation and determines its usefulness to human beings. God's miraculous power is revealed in His creation and is in everything we eat.

Then we can think about and be thankful for all the people involved; every meal you eat probably required the labor of at least 1000 people (In time robots will take over all of the steps of production but food itself and what happens within you will still be pretty miraculous). Think it backwards: the production of your bowl of Frosted Flakes for example started long before the moment the corn flakes were sprayed with sugar and boxed into boxes, long before the corn seeds were planted in the earth, long before the farm supply companies sold the seed to the farmer. Someone pumped the oil out of the ground that someone refined to make the oil and gas to power the trucks that transported every seed and the tractors that planted and the harvesters that harvested, and before that someone build the factories that made every tool. Before that someone generated the power for the factories and someone produced the raw materials that went into the production of the machines, and so on.

We can go back and back until we finally get to God who made the creation, but even in the short term, one set of farmers grew the sugar cane to make the sugar that covers your frosted flakes and another grew the corn, and another farmer raised the cattle that produced the milk, and so on and so on. At every step there were middlemen who bought and sold the raw materials, the giant factories that churned out box after box of frosted flakes were staffed with people, and someone had to manufacture the giant factory machines and so on. We don't think about all that as we pour the flakes into our bowl, but if we would pause to think of all that goes into the production of one bowl of cereal, all the people involved in getting onto our table, you can see why I said that over 1000 people had a hand in getting your bowl of Frosted Flakes. I think it is pretty miraculous, don't you? It is both miraculous and something to be thankful to God for.

After centering our minds in bringing attention to the miracles that the food we are about to eat represents, we take a moment to imagine that you are eating in the presence of Jesus. Picture how he would eat, how he would approach the meal, and you want to eat in a way with him that will not embarrass you in front of him. Now, pause for another brief prayer to give God thanks for all that went into the production of your food, and lift up those around the world who will not know a full stomach this day; thank God for sustaining our lives through food and you are ready to begin eating.

As you eat, eat somewhat slowly taking each bite as an event, and paying attention to each taste. Pick out each of the flavors; think about the texture – is it crunchy or soft or chewy? If so, what makes it so? Is it hot or cold or warm, and what part of your tongue is getting the most out of it? Chew as slowly as you can comfortably do, and if your mind wanders then, just as if you were praying and your mind wandered to other thoughts, when you realize it bring your attention back to the food you are eating.

Pause mid-meal to thank God remembering that every bit of what you are eating is your mouth by the grace of God. How does whatever you are drinking with the meal hit your tongue? Pay attention to how it feels as well. Lastly since Jesus is watching us, you don't want to embarrass yourself by overeating, so stop as soon as you are no longer hungry (not when you are stuffed to the point of immobility). At the end of the meal take time to thank God again, for this gift of food from his hand. Think again briefly of the miracles involved in getting food onto your plate, and of how enjoyable each mouthful was and we acknowledge in prayer that each bit of food and drink, each taste and texture is an expression of God's love for you, and that you are grateful for it all.

Because I was writing about this subject in the middle of the day, on my lunch break I did this exercise while I sat at my desk eating a Taco Bell chalupa and some potato salad. I was really surprised at how much fun it was! Most of the time I take about five minutes for lunch; I eat some quick thing without paying much attention at all to the food, while I catch up with the day's news on the computer. When I think about eating lunch, I think about it as filling up the gas tank with fuel, instead of as a reward and a blessing and joy. But now I was mindful about my meal: the chalupa was hot and crunchy in some parts, soft in others and chewy in others. It was a bit salty and I hadn't realized what a great mix of textures and flavors are in a chalupa. I paid attention and as I chewed, I could feel the difference between the beef and the tomato and lettuce and the shell. Then I thought about the wheat growing in the fields and how long it took to grow from seed to wheat and what steps and processes the wheat had to go through to get into my chalupa. I was aware of the spices I could taste and the coolness of the sour cream. The potato salad I noticed was cold and mild compared to the chalupa, and I started to wonder, where were these potatoes grown, and what were the crunchy parts in the salad in it made of? And then I paid attention to the cold water I washed it down with. It was so refreshing, and I appreciated the way it cleared all the flavors off my tongue; and when I took a big gulp of water, I could feel it go all the way down. All these were things I normally would have paid no attention to, but now I was thankful for each.

My conclusion was: "Wow, this is great! I have to do this more often!" Now obviously it would be difficult to do this kind of exercise if you are eating a burger in your car while driving across town, in a busy office, at a restaurant with family or friends, or even at home if you live with other people, but it as often as you can find the time for it you will be blessed. Bringing a high level of mindfulness to my lunch turned it into a joyful spiritual experience. It was joyful because it really made me appreciate my meal so much more than I normally would. It was spiritual because it made me so thankful to God and really appreciative of my many blessings. A side benefit to this exercise also emerged: I found that I ate less because I was eating slower and felt full sooner. I read a testimonial online from a guy who wrote that he did a version of Ignatius' exercise at every meal for three months and was thrilled because it caused him to slow down his intake and feel full faster and as a result, he lost 67 pounds!

I want to close this chapter with a quick mention of two other things concerning food and spirituality: fasting, and dieting. Fasting, especially during Lent, is something I do every year. Fasting is the exact opposite of eating food as a spiritual exercise: fasting is about not eating any food, or not eating some specific food item, such as bread or sugar, as a way to focus one's attention on God. There are several Biblical examples: Queen Esther asked for the Jews of Susa to fast for her for three days, to support her application to her husband the King to spare the Jews (Esther 4:16); and when Judah was threatened by an invasion of the Ammonites and Moabites King Jehoshaphat proclaimed a fast (2 Chronicles 20:3).

Fasting works as a spiritual exercise in this way, every time that you feel hungry you think of God and give a short prayer of praise or thanks for some aspect of God's love or provision in your life. During Lent I usually give up all sweets to remind myself to be thankful for the bitterness of what Jesus suffered on the cross. Every time I am hungry during Lent or craving a sweet, I say a prayer of thanks to Jesus for what he suffered for me; this helps me to pray much more often during the day than I normally would. I find that thinking so much about Jesus suffering also helps me focus on Easter as the joy of the resurrection.

Lastly, I want to say a word about obesity and dieting. In Ecclesiastes (9:7 NLT) we read: "So go ahead. Eat your food with joy, and drink your wine with a happy heart, for God approves of this!" The truth is that while God approves for us to enjoy our food and drink with happy hearts (which is great), God also does not approve of self-destruction. The apostle Paul twice reminded us that our bodies are temples of the Holy Spirit. He was speaking in the context of avoiding sexual sin, but the analogy also applies to overeating. The temple of our body is only as strong as its walls, floors and roof. What we put into our mouths directly affects the temple maintenance. Anorexia and other forms of under eating weaken the walls of the temple. Gluttony is a sin that affects the body worse in some ways than sexual sins can; it undermines the whole foundation of the temple, with hypertension and diabetes the inevitable result.

Eating is a natural a basic need, a normal desire and a healthy impulse for us. The problem for many of us, me included, is that because food tastes good, because we are not being mindful about the messages that our bodies are sending that we have taken in enough, and because the feeling of being stuffed is a comforting feeling, it is very easy to over eat and thus put on unneeded and unwanted weight. In the pre-industrial age, humans generally had to work hard to get and prepare food - a reality reflected in the Bible. God told Adam (Genesis 3:19) that, "as a result of his sin you will eat by the sweat of your brow." Our bodies adapted to living in harsh conditions over eons of human evolution to become incredibly efficient. We can all live and function normally for at least two days with no water, with water alone we can live for weeks.

Our bodies were made for the days when we were hunter gatherers and food supplies were unreliable. Now we have to work almost as hard as pre-industrial people did in getting their food, to maintain a healthy weight, or to lose the extra weight we have put on that will cause health problems if we don't get rid of it. As a result, many of us have a love hate relationship with food: we love food, and love to eat, but we hate what it does to us when we are not careful. The apostle Paul wrote: "whether you eat or drink, or whatever you do, do it all for the glory of God." Eating with greater awareness is part of an overall plan for our healthiness that can help us to grow in our relationship with God. If we will pause to say thanks before every meal, and if we will be mindful while we eat of the miracles that food represents, both of those things will strengthen our relationship with God. And I am sure if you eat mindfully consistently, you will find what I have found: mindfulness has slowed down my eating, allowed me to enjoy food a lot more, and at the same time caused me to eat at least a little less then I otherwise would have, and thus manage my weight more easily. Again, how great it is that we can take something we do three times a day and make it an important way to help us build our relationship with God into something great.

Let us pray:

> Lord, everything I have has come to me through Your hand. How often I forget to thank You for providing food, the most basic of my needs; or to give even a thought to the miracles that each

bite represents. I thank You Lord for that goes into the production of my food, for those who grow, produce, transport, sell and prepare my food. Lord You feed the birds and I know I am more important to You than they are; so help me I pray to trust that You will provide for me. Lord You have given me a nose to smell and a tongue to taste the rich bounty of Your good earth. Help me always remember to give thanks to You at mealtimes and while eating may I remember our food is a gift of Your love. Thank You Lord for all of this, in Jesus' name. Amen.

Scripture Quotes & Sermon Notes
The Kitchen

Luke 6:47-48 (NLT) 47I will show you what it's like when someone comes to me, listens to my teaching, and then follows it. 48It is like a person building a house who digs deep and lays the foundation on solid rock. When the floodwaters rise and break against the house, it stands firm because it is well built.

Psalms 23:5 (KJV) Thou preparest a table before me in the presence of mine enemies: thou anointest my head with oil; my cup runneth over.

Psalms 59:10 (TEV) My God loves me and will come to me; he will let me see my enemies defeated.

Matthew 6:26 (NLT) 26Look at the birds. They don't plant or harvest or store food in barns, for your heavenly Father feeds them. And aren't you far more valuable to him than they are?... 33Seek the Kingdom of God above all else, and live righteously, and he will give you everything you need.

Ecclesiastes 3:13 (NLT) 13And people should eat and drink and enjoy the fruits of their labor, for these are gifts from God.

1 Corinthians 10:31 (NLT) So whether you eat or drink, or whatever you do, do it all for the glory of God.

Spiritual Exercise with Food

1. Find time for the exercise when and where you can be alone or at least in a part of the house where you can be by yourself.

2. Get rid of all distractions by turning off the TV and the phone.

3. Prepare a cold meal.

4. Start by giving God the thanks for miracle of the food and for all those who had a hand in the food in front of you; lifting up also those around the world who will not know a full stomach tonight; and for the miraculous way that your body that is sustained through food. Lastly ask God for the help of His Spirit to complete this exercise and to be blessed by it.

5. Imagine that you are eating in the presence of Jesus and you want to impress him with how mindful you are. Be mindful also of how he would eat.

6. Take moderate to small sized bites, chew slowly enough to allow you to pay attention to each taste. In every bite pick out each of the flavors, think about the texture – is it crunchy or soft or chewy? If so why? Is it hot or cold or warm, and what part of your tongue is getting the most out of it? How does whatever you are drinking with the meal hit your tongue? Where was it grown? Where was it processed and by whom?

7. Pause and thank God from time to time during the meal because every bit of what you are eating is your mouth by the grace of God.

8. If your mind wanders while eating then just as if you were praying and your mind wandered to other thoughts, when you realize you've become distracted bring your attention back to the food you are eating.

9. Since Jesus is watching you, you don't want to embarrass yourself by overeating, so stop as soon as your hunger is gone.

10. At the end of the meal take time to thank God again for this gift of the extravagant bounty of food you have enjoyed from his hand, remembering that each meal is an expression of His love for you.

Chapter Fourteen: The Servants' Quarters

Originally preached June 9, 2019

When my wife Anna and I lived in Hong Kong we were lucky enough to live in a luxury apartment (subsidized by her employer) that was so large that it included servants' quarters. The kitchen had attached to it two bedrooms, presumably one room for the maid and one for the nanny, and there was a separate bathroom, and entrance, and a private elevator for the servants. How much more so would a palace have large servants' quarters? In our spiritual palace there are no servants' quarters because we are servants, and the whole palace is a servant's quarters. Remember I said earlier that no one else can live in your spiritual palace but you, that each person must build their own relationship with God. So if you own a spiritual palace relationship with God you are automatically both servant and maintenance man or woman.

One of the key expectations Jesus has of his disciples is that we all are expected to serve God as a part of the practice of our faith; if we don't serve God, I don't believe we can be pleasing to God. This is the bar that Jesus set:

> "the rulers in this world lord it over their people, and officials flaunt their authority over those under them. This, however, is not the way it shall be among you. If one of you wants to be great, you must be the servant of the rest;"

By being a servant Jesus meant that we should give our time and energy to serving others as our way of honoring God and as part of our obedience to God. Obviously, if we cannot accomplish greatness unless we serve, that also means we cannot build a spiritual palace relationship with God without serving.

Serving is so vital to building a close relationship with God for several reasons: first, serving reflects a humility and willingness to be obedient that is an indication of openness to God, without which we cannot succeed in building up our relationship with God. Serving others, even if done purely to please God, generally reorients the mind and heart in alignment with God's will and intentions for the server. Openness to God and willingness to be obedient through serving others, also helps produce Godly attitudes of humility and compassion that are each also essential to attaining higher levels of relationship with God. So us serving others is important to God because it helps us get closer to God.

In the rest of this chapter I am going to give a brief Biblical survey of what God has said about us serving God and about the spiritual gifts God has given believers in Jesus Christ to equip us to serve. I am also going to talk about why and how serving others is good for us physically, mentally, and emotionally, and how the combination of all these things helps us build up our relationship with God into a stronger spiritual palace.

Would you join me in a prayer?

> Lord God, I thank You that in Your word You told us that You are a God of love. I thank You for Your love, for me and for the world. I thank You Lord that because You are love and because You are power, the power of the universe is love. So I pray that You would pour out on me now the power of the universe – pour out on me Your love; surround me with Your love until I find myself completely immersed in Your love. While I am immersed in Your love

let Your love also flow through every pore in my body, let Your love flow between my every atom. I pray that I may serve in Your love, and in my service may I grow in my love for You.

President Woodrow Wilson wrote: "There is no higher religion than human service. To work for the common good is the greatest creed." To me the highest religion is faith in God through Jesus Christ, but I believe President Wilson is correct that "to work for the common good is the greatest creed." The apostle Paul said something similar in his letter to the Romans (12:1): "serving God is true worship." And Jesus said that the second greatest commandment is to love our neighbors as ourselves, and we may infer from that commandment an expectation that we put our love into action through serving others.

As Christians we are also inheritors of the Old Testament admonitions to serve God and serve others. Many Jewish scholars have argued that Jesus taught nothing new, that everything he taught is found in the Old Testament. While that is easily disproved by Jesus', "You have heard…" statements, it is true that very much of what he taught is taken from the Old Testament, and that virtually everything he said or did is in some way related to the Old Testament (OT). In the OT book of Deuteronomy we read: "So now, O Israel, what does the LORD your God require of you? Only to fear the LORD your God, to walk in all his ways, to love him, <u>to serve the LORD your God with all your heart and with all your soul</u>" (Deut. 10:12 NRSV). Indeed the Old Testament repeatedly tells us to love and to serve God and in fact, warns us against failing to serve the Lord:

> "<u>If you do not serve the LORD your God</u> with joy and enthusiasm for the abundant benefits you have received, 48you will serve your enemies whom the LORD will send against you. You will be left hungry, thirsty, naked, and lacking in everything.

> The LORD will put an iron yoke on your neck, oppressing you harshly until he has destroyed you. (Deuteronomy 28:47-48 NLT)

How do we serve with joy and enthusiasm when we might rather watch a drama on TV? We serve with joy and enthusiasm because our thankfulness compels us, when we realize that the value of all we have been given by God so drastically outweighs the time we give to God in service.

Another difference between the Old and New Testament is that in the Old Testament the call to service is more focused on obedience to God's laws while in the New Testament service to God is more focused on serving other people in God's name while. There is no precedence or equivalence in the Old Testament for the three different times that Jesus instructed his disciples, 'if you want to be great, you must be a servant of others' (Matthew 20:25-28 on the road to Jerusalem, Mark 9:33-36 at Capernaum, Luke 9:37-43 by the Mount of Transfiguration).

One of the more famous stories about Jesus' disciples is the passage from Matthew 20: the mother of Jesus disciples James and John came to Jesus with her sons to ask a favor: "In your Kingdom, please let my two sons sit in places of honor next to you, one on your right and the other on your left." When the rest of the disciples hear about this, they were angry, and Jesus used it as a teaching moment. According to the Gospels he had already taught them this lesson twice before but maybe this time because they were angry, he got their attention. He told them again, "If you want to be great, you must be the servant of all the others. And if you want to be first, you must be the slave of the rest."

I found as I was looking at how several different versions of the Bible translate this verse, I found that some versions don't use the word *slave*, they just use the word *servant* throughout. I found that the Contemporary English Version translates it accurately from the Greek:

> "If you want to be great, you must be the servant [diakoneo] (from which we get our word deacon) of all the others. And if you want to be first you must be the slave [doulos] of the rest. For even the Son of Man came not to be served [diakoneo] but to serve [diakoneo] others and to give his life as a ransom for many."
> **(Matthew 20:26-27, 45)**

The Greek words help us to see that Jesus came to serve us but not to be our slave. They also help us to see that Jesus sets a very high bar for our service: service to the point of self-enslavement.

I find it interesting that while Jesus set a high bar of service for those who want to be great disciples, he did not spell out for us in so many words how to serve. Jesus does not, in any of the Gospels, give us a list of ways to serve. Instead he gives us examples of service for us to follow such as these: "blessed are the peace makers for they will be called children of God… Blessed are those who hunger and thirst for righteousness…" and "whatever you do for the least of these my children you do for me."[2] Jesus also gave us several examples of his own serving of others, the most obvious being his washing of the disciples' feet, followed by the feeding of the crowds: 4000 one time and 5000 another.

> Taking the five loaves and the two fish, he looked up to heaven, and blessed and broke the loaves, and gave them to his disciples to set before the people; and he divided the two fish among them all. And all ate and were filled; and they took up twelve

---

[2] Matthew 5:6,9, and 25:40.

baskets full of broken pieces and of the fish. Those who had eaten the loaves numbered five thousand men. **(Mark 6:41-44 NRSV)**

Feeding 5000 people with a few loaves of bread was not a "wave of the hand and done" miracle. The Gospels tell us Jesus performed the miracle by breaking the loaves up into enough pieces to feed 5000 people. On communion Sundays I take a loaf of bread and break it as part of the communion ritual; I know from years of practice exactly how long it takes to rip a good-sized loaf of bread in half. I estimate about one second per rip, times five thousand, plus breaking up the fish, that could have been 1 ½ to 2 hours of what must have been pretty exhausting serving.

I think also about Jesus service of healing for the sick. As He became more and more famous crowds of people (like the 5000 He fed) followed him pushing to get to Him, many sick people calling out to him trying to touch him to be healed by Him, like the woman who was bleeding for twelve years until she touched Him. Matthew reported people would gather from throughout the region to come to Jesus for healing and Jesus would heal them all (Matthew 14:35-36 NRSV). Jesus served by allowing himself to be used as a spiritual faucet pouring out the healing power of God on those he touched. And of course He gave His life in service, suffering and dying for us. His life was spent just as he told His disciples, as one who came to serve.

Jesus gave us only examples of service, but Paul did give us several lists of ways we can serve in his description of the spiritual gifts (Romans 12:3-6, Ephesians 4:2-12, and 1 Corinthians 12:1-31). Paul tells us that the Holy Spirit gives every believer a spiritual gift that He chooses for them; Paul explains: "A spiritual gift is given to each of us *so we can help each other*." This will not be news to most of readers, but God has given each one of us at least one gift *so that we can serve*. The fact that God equips each of us to serve, by giving each of us a gift or gifts to help us serve, lets us know how important it is to God that we serve people in God's name. He not only calls us to serve, He equips us so that we can serve better.

A quick Google search for "spiritual gifts tests" will reveal many free "tests" that generally test for up to twenty-five spiritual gifts, that have been identified in one of Paul's lists. However, these twenty-five gifts are just the gifts the apostle names; truly there are many different spiritual gifts not listed in the Bible. It seems that everyone gets at least one of these Biblically listed twenty-five gifts, but most people get something like a gift cluster: gifts that go together, like preaching and teaching, or charity and hospitality.

If you take a spiritual gift test online my recommendation is that you take it with a grain of salt. I have a very gifted friend who was greatly discouraged because when he took a spiritual gifts assessment it only listed him as having one of the gifts - music. I know for a fact that he also has the gift of administration, but the test did not indicate so. He took the assessment as a part of a group of prospective lay ministers who were all taking the test together. Afterwards they all shared their results with each other, all the others had several and some had as many as twenty of the gifts. My friend was embarrassed at only having one identified gift and so he dropped out of the program, but I know that he would have done well if he stayed.

The Apostle Peter said (1 Peter 4:10 NLT), "God has given each of you a gift from his *great variety* of spiritual gifts. Use them well to serve one another." "Great variety of gifts" certainly implies more than twenty-five; so the tests are useful but there are many ways to serve and many gifts that the Bible does not list. A spiritual gift is revealed in this: you set out to use your talents, abilities and interests to serve God by serving others, and while you are serving, God comes along side you through the inspiration of the Holy Spirit, and helps you by lifting your performance or enhancing your ability to help, beyond what you could do without God's help.

One of the gifts I have that is not in one of Paul's lists is the gift of writing. Many a time over the years I have had a particularly busy week serving God and as a result sermon preparation for Sunday morning gets pushed all the way back to Saturday afternoon! I do my best in the short time available, humbly offering myself to God, and asking for His help. The next morning I give the sermon with trepidation, but many people comment to me afterwards that the sermon touched them and that it was inspired. I know that it must have been inspired, that God blessed my mess. Literally, God helped me write and find the words and aided the delivery so that His people were blessed through me. And God often reveals His handiwork by giving me confirmations: the choir director has picked three hymns that all go with my sermon without know what I was speaking on. The associate pastor wrote a pastoral prayer that emphasizes my sermon's main points without knowing what I was going to talk about, and someone will come up to me after church and tell me that my sermon spoke to them and helped them with an issue they were struggling with. That kind of multiple confirmation happens frequently.

Every one of us has an area of giftedness that we can use to serve God by serving others. A musician can offer her performance to God and realizes afterwards that she has given a 'gifted' performance; a counselor prays and gets supernaturally revealed insight into a couple's problems and finds words that bring immediate healing; a teacher prays and is able to get through to a difficult or challenging student; a surgeon performs a delicate surgery perfectly and so on. We need to set out to serve others as our way to serve God and God comes along side us with the Holy Spirit to help us help.

Now among the spiritual gifts that Paul mentions are wisdom, knowledge, faith, miracles, prophetic speech, and discernment.

These gifts don't require us to do physical labor to serve; instead they come in handy for counseling and encouraging. The mission trips I have gone on all required serving in some sort of physical labor, and that too can certainly be a spiritual gift; but counseling and encouraging are things a person can do on their death bed. So regardless of our age, gender or physical limitations, any one of us can, and every one of us is called to, serve God by using our gift or gifts to serve others.

Movie star and former governor of California Arnold Schwarzenegger donated his entire salary as governor to various charities, and he is currently a spokesman for the Special Olympics. He said this: "Help others and give something back. I guarantee you will discover that while public service improves the lives and the world around you, its greatest reward is the enrichment and new meaning it will bring your own life." Arnold is 100% correct: like so many of the things that God instructs us to do, serving others rewards us physically, mentally, emotionally and spiritually.

Studies of older adults have found that retirees experience greater benefits from their own volunteering than people who are not yet retired. If you go online and do a Google search as I did, ask: "is serving others good for you?" you will find, as I did, dozens of scientific studies have been completed that tell us that serving others is very good for you. One study I read said that if you volunteer 200 hours a year or more it decreases your risk of hypertension by a whopping forty percent. Serving others on a regular basis also improves your ability to manage stress, it improves your resistance to diseases, it releases chemicals in your brain that make you feel joyful and that fight off depression; and in general, helping others increases your satisfaction with life. When you help others you become more thankful for what you have that you can help others with; and joy and peace are byproducts of thankfulness. That is a good example of God's economy in action – when you show love and compassion and charity by serving others you are blessed in many ways in return.

There is an old Biblically based saying that: "Charity begins at home." That saying means that the best place to serve others is in the place you are, and with the people you are closest to in your family and in your workplace. If you are married you can serve by using the gifts of patience, compassion, forgiveness and emotional support. In your workplace you can serve by encouraging and praying for your co-workers. You can serve your neighbors by bringing over a dish or helping with some chore. And of course at and through church there are many ways to serve by giving of your time and talents and resources. One last cool benefit of serving others I want to mention - researchers at UCLA found, and I quote: "When we see someone else help another person it gives us a good feeling, which in turn causes us to go out and do something altruistic ourselves." In other words serving others is contagious, when someone sees you giving your service to someone else it encourages the observer to also serve, and so the circle of love and happiness expands.

What are your spiritual gifts? If you want to familiarize yourself with the whole range of gifts and confirm to yourself what gifts God has given you my recommendation is that you find one of the many different free spiritual gift's tests online. In the meantime let me wat that we tend to naturally drift towards doing the things that we enjoy, and at the same time that bring us appreciation; and those things we enjoy and are appreciated for generally reveal the gifts that we have. If you already know what gifts God has given you, or when you take the assessment and learn your gifts, then I want to encourage you - whatever gifts you have, give in to the temptation to serve others with them. Find a time and a place to serve and make a commitment to do so. You will find that when you give in to the temptation to serve others you will be greatly blessed as you seek to be a blessing to others.

So in this chapter we have heard that God is calling every one of us to serve others; that God has given us spiritual gifts to help us serve; and that serving others is good for us mentally, physically and emotionally. Mentally, serving helps us to stay sharp as we age; emotionally, serving fights depression and makes us feel more positive about life; and physically serving helps lower our blood pressure and helps us live longer. Our mental, physical and emotional healthiness contributes to our spiritual healthiness by removing challenges to our relationship with God that unhealthiness in any of these areas brings. Serving others also helps you build up your relationship with God by making you feel appreciative for what you have and thus you feel more joy filled and at peace.

Jesus promised: "My Father will honor anyone who serves me", so I am going to close this chapter by asking you to join me committing together in prayer with me to serve God more and better.

> Lord God You have given each of us a gift from Your great variety of spiritual gifts, and You have told us Father to use whatever You have given us to serve one another well. Fan the flames of the spiritual gifts You have given me, especially the gift of faith, and love towards others and I will serve with all the strength and energy that You supply me. Then everything I do in serving will bring glory to You God through Jesus Christ our Lord. All glory and power to You Father, Son and Holy Spirit, now forever and ever! Amen.

Questions for Self-Reflection

- Do you know what your spiritual gifts are?

- Have you used your spiritual gifts to serve?

- If so, how was your service received?

- Are there any gifts you don't have but would like to have and if so, have you prayed about it?

- Do you make a point of making time for serving other people?

Scripture Quotes : Servants' Quarters

Romans 12:1 (TEV) ¹So then, my friends, because of God's great mercy to us I appeal to you: Offer yourselves as a living sacrifice to God, dedicated to his service and pleasing to him. This is the true worship that you should offer.

Deuteronomy 10:12-13 (NRSV) ¹²So now, O Israel, what does the LORD your God require of you? Only to fear the LORD your God, to walk in all his ways, to love him, to serve the LORD your God with all your heart and with all your soul, ¹³and to keep the commandments of the LORD your God and his decrees that I am commanding you today, for your own well-being.

Luke 4:8 (NLT) Jesus replied, "The Scriptures say, 'You must worship the LORD your God and serve only him.'"

Matthew 20:25-28 (CEV) 25 But Jesus called the disciples together and said: You know that foreign rulers like to order their people around. And their great leaders have full power over everyone they rule. 26 But don't act like them. If you want to be great, (megos) you must be the servant (diakonos) of all the others. 27And if you want to be first (protos), you must be the slave (dulos) of the rest. 45For even the Son of Man came not to be served (diakonos) but to serve (diakonos) others and to give his life as a ransom for many."

1 Corinthians 12:4-7 (TEV) ⁴There are different kinds of spiritual gifts, but the same Spirit gives them. ⁵There are different ways of serving, but the same Lord is served. ⁶There are different abilities to perform service, but the same God gives ability to all for their particular service. (1 Corinthians 12:7 NLT) <u>A spiritual gift is given to each of us so we can help each other.</u>

John 12:26 (TEV) ²⁶Whoever wants to serve me must follow me, so that my servant will be with me where I am. And <u>my Father will honor anyone who serves me.</u>

1 Peter 4:10-11 (NLT) ¹⁰<u>God has given each of you a gift from his great variety of spiritual gifts.</u> <u>Use them well to serve one another.</u> ¹¹Do you have the gift of speaking? Then speak as though God himself were speaking through you. Do you have the gift of helping others? Do it with all the strength and energy that God supplies. Then everything you do will bring glory to God through Jesus Christ. All glory and power to him forever and ever! Amen.

OTHER HELPFUL VERSES ON SERVING NOT QUOTED IN THE SERMON

Psalms 100:2 (NKJV) Serve the LORD with gladness; Come before His presence with singing.

Romans 7:5-6 (NLT) ⁵When we were controlled by our old nature, sinful desires were at work within us, and the law aroused these evil desires that produced a harvest of sinful deeds, resulting in death. ⁶But now we have been released from the law, for we died to it and are no longer captive to its power. Now we can serve God, not in the old way of obeying the letter of the law, but in the new way of living in the Spirit.

Deuteronomy 11:13 (TEV) "So then, obey the commands that I have given you today; love the Lord your God and <u>serve him with all your heart.</u>

Deuteronomy 28:47-48 (NLT) <u>⁴⁷If you do not serve the LORD your God with joy and enthusiasm for the abundant benefits you have received</u>, 48you will serve your enemies whom the LORD will send against you. You will be left hungry, thirsty, naked, and lacking in everything. The LORD will put an iron yoke on your neck, oppressing you harshly until he has destroyed you.

Psalms 2:10-12 (NLT) 10 Now then, you kings, act wisely! Be warned, you rulers of the earth! <u>Serve the LORD with reverent fear and rejoice with trembling.</u>12 Submit to God's royal son, or he will become angry, and you will be destroyed in the midst of all your activities—for his anger flares up in an instant. But what joy for all who take refuge in him!

Luke 17:7-10 (CEV) 7If your servant comes in from plowing or from taking care of the sheep, would you say, "Welcome! Come on in and have something to eat"? 8No, you wouldn't say that. You would say, "Fix me something to eat. Get ready to serve me, so I can have my meal. Then later on you can eat and drink." 9Servants don't deserve special thanks for doing what they are supposed to do. 10And that's how it should be with you. When you've done all you should, then say, <u>"We are merely servants, and we have simply done our duty."</u>

Matthew 23:11-12 (NLT) <u>11The greatest among you must be a servant</u>. 12But those who exalt themselves will be humbled, and those who humble themselves will be exalted.

Mark 9:33-35 (NLT) ³³After they arrived at Capernaum and settled in a house, Jesus asked his disciples, "What were you discussing out on the road?" ³⁴But they didn't answer because they had been arguing about which of them was the greatest. ³⁵He sat down, called the twelve disciples over to him, and said, <u>"Whoever wants to be first must take last place and be the servant of everyone else."</u>

Chapter Fifteen: Spiritual Maintenance

Originally preached June 23, 2019

When I say maintenance what do you think of? I think of the tasks I help with often around church: setting up tables and chairs, fixing holes in the roof, killing wasps etc. I think about the same floors being swept and washed again and again, and the endless variety of things that break, leak or need replacing or replenishing. Maintenance is not a glamorous job, but I have found over the years that career maintenance men, are as a rule, good and humble people, and far more knowledgeable than we might give them credit for. If you have not spent any time serving at your church, even if your gifts lie elsewhere, volunteering a few hours to help the maintenance person will probably be a blessing to you.

In this chapter I am going to talk about three kinds of spiritual maintenance: cleaning, preventative maintenance, and repairing that which is broken or damaged. But before I go on would you join me in prayer?

> Lord God I thank You for the awesome privilege and responsibility of working to build my relationship with You into a spiritual palace. Building my palace I know is so good for me and it is also so good for the others in my life as my service, goodness and integrity are inspiring to those I care about and contagious to those who observe me in action. So help me continue to better do the important work of spiritual maintenance through this chapter. Thank You Lord! Amen.

The reality is that in this modern day and age every one of us has become something of a maintenance man or a maintenance woman. We each have so many things that we maintain: of course we maintain our health, we maintain our teeth and our appearance, and we maintain our clothes. If you own a smart phone you have to maintain it – keep the screen clean, the battery charged, and the apps and software up to date. For those of us who own a car we have to maintain our cars, and if we own a home, we have lots of things to maintain, the yard, the AC system and so on. You are already a maintainer of so many things that I don't want to add another thing for you to maintain, but I do need to point out that the most important thing in your life to maintain is your spirituality, your relationship with God.

Spiritual maintenance can easy to overlook but I can give you several good reasons why your spirituality is the most important part of your life to maintain. First of all life is so uncertain, any one of us can be gone tomorrow, or later on today. I own a motorcycle and as I was driving in the right lane down the street that runs in front of my church a man in the left lane did not see me and started to move into my lane as I was beside him. Fortunately I was able to see what was happening in time and jam on the brakes to get out of his way, but if I had not, I would have been run off the road into some trees at 45 miles per hour. It was a timely reminder to me that any of us can be taken pretty much at any time, so we need to do the work of maintaining our spirituality so that we are prepared at any time to meet our maker.

In his parable of the ten bridesmaids, five of whom were wise and five who were foolish, Jesus' conclusion was, "keep awake" - be prepared because "you know neither the day nor the hour of my return." Whether it is Jesus coming to us or, apparently more likely us going to him, we need to be ready at all times; and that is the most important part of spiritual maintenance – being ready to meet Jesus. Second, your spirituality is important to maintain because, as I mentioned several times in previous chapters, spiritual healthiness contributes to your physical, mental and emotional health. Thirdly, maintaining a good relationship with God is pleasing to God; how often do you do something that you know is truly pleasing to God? And lastly, maintaining a good relationship with God changes your attitude towards everything else in your life.

I remember the days before I had a strong relationship with God: my life was confusing, and chaotic; I was trying unsuccessfully to figure out what my purpose in life was, and I became very depressed. I thought about suicide almost daily for about two years until getting a relationship with God changed my life. Developing a relationship with God was like needing glasses for my whole life and finally putting on a pair of glasses and suddenly everything in life is in focus. Over the years my experiences with God and my resultant knowledge of God have continually grown to the point where now I not only understand my purpose and the purpose of life, but everything in my life flows from that one important point. I know that God is my Creator and Father, and that Jesus is my Lord and Savior, and the Holy Spirit is God with me and within me. One of my favorite Methodist hymns says, "Because he lives, I can face tomorrow, because he lives all fear is gone… and life is worth the living just because he lives." If the words of that hymn describe your relationship with God, then you know how a relationship with God reshapes your life and brings everything in your life into focus and perspective; if not then you owe it to yourself to find out how to get there.

Now as I said there are three kinds of maintenance: the maintenance of cleaning; preventative maintenance; and the maintenance of repairing that which is broken, damaged, or worn out, and we need to do all three kinds of maintenance in maintaining our spiritual palace relationship with God. When we come to a church, we have an expectation that the floors and grounds will be clean and that there will be soap in the dispensers, and toilet paper stocked and so on. So cleaning is the first maintenance responsibility in a church. In the same way, keeping our spiritual palace clean is our first spiritual maintenance. By clean I mean it in the same sense as a referee who calls the fighters to the center of the ring in a boxing match and tells them he wants a "clean fight."

For a boxer that means they will obey the rules while they pummel each other. For us keeping it clean means doing our best to obey or keep God's rules, including the Ten Commandments, while we fight the good fight of life. Most of us are good about nine of the commandments: we don't worship other God's or make idols, we don't use the Lord's name in vain (some of us still need work on that), we honor our mom & dad, we are not committing adultery or murdering anyone, but the place most people fall short is keeping the Sabbath day. Keeping the Sabbath day holy is an interesting commandment because it falls into all three types of maintenance. Keeping the Sabbath day holy helps us stay clean in the sense that is a part of obeying the rules of God, and keeping the Sabbath day is also part of our regular spiritual maintenance helping us keep our relationship with God strong, and it is also helpful for repairing a damaged or broken relationship which I will talk about in a few minutes. First, I want to talk about preventative maintenance.

In the church I serve our maintenance man is John Payne.; John is a humble man with a good heart. In addition to keeping the church clean his next major responsibility is preventative maintenance. He keeps a written record of what he does and when he does it, so that the windows in our glass doors get cleaned weekly, the air filters get changed every other month, and the AC drain line gets flushed quarterly, and certain bulbs get changed annually. In the same way, in your relationship with God, preventative maintenance is the smart thing to do to prevent larger problems in the future. Your preventative maintenance schedule might include, daily prayer, daily Bible reading, weekly worship attendance, monthly service, and annual examination of conscience.

It is very significant that Jesus said this at the end of His Sermon on the Mount:

> "Everyone then who hears these words of mine and acts on them will be like a wise man who built his house on rock. The rain fell, the floods came, and the winds blew and beat on that house, but it did not fall, because it had been founded on rock." (Matthew 7:24-27 NRSV)

Listening to Jesus' words and obeying them is preventative spiritual maintenance: it is getting ready for what you know is coming. Building a house on a rock is getting ready for that storm you know is coming. The poet Henry Wadsworth Longfellow wrote, "into every life some rain must fall" but in my experience it is not some rain; into every life a giant storm is going to happen, and probably also a hurricane, and maybe even a flood will happen. I sincerely doubt that anyone reading this has not already gone through one storm in your life, but if you haven't, I assure you a storm is in your future. So listening to Jesus words and obeying them is spiritual maintenance – getting ready for the storms we know are coming.

One of Jesus' most famous sayings is, "I am the vine and you are the branches, if you remain in me and my words remain in you, you may ask for anything you want, and it will be granted!" That also is about the spiritual maintenance of doing the things we need to do to stay attached to the vine. That last statement of Jesus - if we stay attached to the vine, we can ask for anything and it will be granted should come with an asterisk or a footnote. The apostle James provides the proviso: "You ask and do not receive, because you ask wrongly, in order to spend what you get on your pleasures." So we need to remain attached to the vine and what we ask has to be within God's will and serve God's purposes. Unfortunately, being attached to the vine does not prevent you from asking for the wrong purposes.

So what kind of regular spiritual maintenance should we be doing? Of course the main and most important part of our spiritual maintenance is prayer. Because God is spirit and we are physical we need to work to open and keep open the channel of communication between the physical realm and the spiritual realm. You may remember that the North Pole is located in the middle of the Arctic Ocean, amid waters that are almost permanently covered with a thick blanket of sea ice. You may have seen how an icebreaker ship breaks a path through the arctic sea ice, and how the path behind the icebreaker quickly fills in behind it?

Arctic sea ice is the perfect metaphor for communications with God. Imagine for a moment that the North Pole is God, and our prayers are like the icebreaker, and the ice is all the junk in between us and God. The junk in the way is our thoughts, the many distractions in our lives, our doubts and fears, and any sins in our life. These are the things that when we pray distract us and stop us from truly bringing 100% of our heart and mind to connecting to God. We have to work as hard as an icebreaker to get through all of that junk to create a channel between us and God; the work we need to do is prayer, reflection, repentance if needed, and still more prayer. Additionally, just as an arctic ice channel fills in quickly with broken pieces of ice and closes up behind the ship as it passes through, if we don't keep our channel open with regular prayer, it too will close up and require much spiritual work to open it up again.

Going to church regularly is another part of the maintenance plan for our faith. When we are together as a group on Sunday morning we are like many logs in a fireplace: the flames of the Holy Spirit burn more easily and brighter. But when we are away from church, we are like logs removed from the fire – unless the wood is extremely dry it is easy for the flames of the Holy Spirit to burn out. There is also nourishment for our faith that comes to us from receiving the sacrament of Holy Communion which we only can get in church. We also maintain our relationship with God by reading scripture—especially the psalms, and the New Testament. Lastly, I mentioned in the previous chapter how serving others also helps us grow in our relationship with God by increasing our love for God and others. Every time we serve others, we are strengthening our faith in God so that too is preventative maintenance.

John the maintenance man also fixes or repairs a lot of little things around the church: a leaky water fountain, a clogged toilet, and etcetera. Preventative spiritual maintenance is great and important, but even when we are doing every kind of spiritual maintenance right on time, our faith can still be damaged and require maintenance when unforeseen tragedies happen. Even the most mature Christian can find their faith is torn and tattered when an unexpected and undeserved tragedy strikes. I will always remember how my faith was initially shaken while I was leading a mission trip, when I saw the devastation in Pascagoula Mississippi after hurricane Katrina. My faith quickly bounced back, but I have known a number of people over the years who have had a tragedy strike, such as losing a relationship, or a job, or a loved one, or who have had a severe illness or injury strike them, and they got so angry with God that their faith was severely damaged or destroyed.

If we experience damage to our faith from tragedy or erosion, of if we are at a low point spiritually and have never had a strong relationship with God, or if we are helping someone whose faith is weak or damaged; the solution for all these things is the same. Paul writes in his first letter to Timothy:

> "I remind you to fan into flames the spiritual gift God gave you when I laid my hands on you. For God has not given us a spirit of fear and timidity, but of power, love, and self-discipline." (**2 Timothy 1:6**)

Fanning the flames of the spirit inside us is what spiritual maintenance is all about. If you find yourself spiritual dry or in need of building up, then the best place to start is with the Lord's Prayer. Repeat it at least daily and pay attention to each of the words. It is truly a perfect prayer and being of divine origin it retains a supernatural ability to cut through the clutter and bring us into the presence of God. To help with your spiritual maintenance I have placed a spiritual exercise to use with the Lord's Prayer at the end of the chapter.

Repairing a broken or damaged relationship with God reminds me of my childhood friend Erik's sailboat. When I was a kid, living in Long Island New York, my friend Erik's parents had a small wooden Beetle Cat sailboat. They lived in New York City and kept the boat near my grandma's house on Fire Island. They only used the boat in the summer, which in New York is Memorial Day to Labor Day. In the fall they would pull up the boat onto the beach, pull out the mast and flip the boat over and leave it chained to a post on the sand on the beach, and there it would stay through the fall, winter and spring.

Over the winter the wood planks of the boat would dry up and shrink a bit so at the beginning of summer when they put the boat into the water you couldn't use it; it would leak and quickly fill with water and sink almost up to the gunnels. But after about two weeks of being filled with water the wood planks would swell up and push together and the boat would stop leaking. Erik and I would get in, in our bathing suits, and bail that boat out, and for the rest of the summer it would be fine.

That boat is also like our relationship with God, the wood planks are our hearts and souls, and sometimes the circumstances of our lives, or our own bad decisions, can distract us and instead of being swelled with the Holy Spirit in relationship with God, our spirituality is on the beach and our planks dry out so that our little ship sinks in the sea of life. Just like with Erik's boat the solution to healing spiritual damage is to immerse ourselves in the things of God: in church, in praying in reading the Bible, in serving and let Jesus' the living water cause our hearts and souls to swell with love and makes our boat tight again.

So in this chapter we have heard that we are called to three types of spiritual maintenance – keeping clean through obedience, preventative maintenance through prayer, attending church, reading the Bible and serving others in God's name; and reparative maintenance, when our faith has faded or become damaged, by immersing ourselves in the things of God to swell our hearts and souls with love for God. As we end this chapter, I want to leave you with this question: is your heart and soul swelled with the love of God? and if not, what spiritual maintenance do you need to do more of?

Scripture Quotes & Sermon Notes
Spiritual Maintenance
6/23/19

Matthew 25:1-13 (NLT) 1"The Kingdom of Heaven can be illustrated by the story of ten bridesmaids who took their lamps and went to meet the bridegroom. 2Five of them were foolish, and five were wise. 3The five who were foolish didn't take enough olive oil for their lamps, 4but the other five were wise enough to take along extra oil. 6"At midnight they were roused by the shout, 'Look, the bridegroom is coming! Come out and meet him!'... 8Then the five foolish ones asked the others, 'Please give us some of your oil because our lamps are going out.' 9"But the others replied, 'We don't have enough for all of us. Go to a shop and buy some for yourselves.' 10"But while they were gone to buy oil, the bridegroom came. Then those who were ready went in with him to the marriage feast, and the door was locked... 13"So <u>you, too, must keep watch! For you do not know the day or hour of my retur</u>n.

Matthew 7:24-27 (NRSV) 24"Everyone then who <u>hears these words of mine and acts on them</u> will be like a wise man who built his house on rock. 25The rain fell, the floods came, and the winds blew and beat on that house, <u>but it did not fall, because it had been founded on rock</u>. 26And everyone who hears these words of mine and does not act on them will be like a foolish man who built his house on sand. 27The rain fell, and the floods came, and the winds blew and beat against that house, and it fell—and great was its fall!"

Exodus 20:8 (NLT) <u>Remember the Sabbath day, and keep it holy</u>.

John 15:3-7 31"I am the true grapevine, and my Father is the gardener. 4Remain in me, and I will remain in you. For a branch cannot produce fruit if it is severed from the vine, and you cannot be fruitful unless you remain in me… Anyone who does not remain in me is thrown away like a useless branch and withers. Such branches are gathered into a pile to be burned. 7But <u>if you remain in me and my words remain in you, you may ask for anything you want, and it will be granted!</u>

Mark 4:16-19 The seed on the rocky soil represents those who hear the message and immediately receive it with joy. 17But since they don't have deep roots, they don't last long. <u>They fall away as soon as they have problems</u> or are persecuted for believing God's word. 18The seed that fell among the thorns represents others who hear God's word, 19but all too quickly <u>the message is crowded out by the worries of this life, the lure of wealth, and the desire for other things</u>, so no fruit is produced.

2 Timothy 1:6-7 This is why <u>I remind you to fan into flames the spiritual gift God gave you when I laid my hands on you</u>. 7For God has not given us a spirit of fear and timidity, but of power, love, and self-discipline.

John 7:37-39 On the last day, the climax of the festival, Jesus stood and shouted to the crowds, "Anyone who is thirsty may come to me! 38Anyone who believes in me may come and drink! For the Scriptures declare, <u>'Rivers of living water will flow from his heart.</u>'" 39(<u>When he said, "living water," he was speaking of the Spirit, who would be given to everyone believing in him</u>. But the Spirit had not yet been given, because Jesus had not yet entered into his glory.)

2 Corinthians 13:5 <u>Examine yourselves to see if your faith is genuine. Test yourselve</u>s. Surely you know that Jesus Christ is among you; if not, you have failed the test of genuine faith.

A Spiritual Exercise with the Lord's Prayer

Praying the Lord's Prayer daily is the most powerful tool I know for creating and restoring damaged or weak faith. St. Ignatius of Loyola created a spiritual exercise on the Lord's prayer in which we pray the Lord's prayer paying attention to the meaning of each word.

Jesus' prayer is the most perfect and powerful prayer ever written. Each word is packed with many levels of meaning. Think of your spirit as a log and the words of the prayer as carpenter's tools that chip away and form something beautiful. Great souls are not born great, they are born with potential, but they are made great by the discipline of placing themselves in the carpenter's hands through prayer and allowing themselves to be shaped and transformed.

The Lord's Prayer contains or transmits all of the elements of effective prayer that are needed to transform your inner heart to one that is right before God. The most important daily discipline for a person seeking to build a spiritual palace relationship with God is that you pray the Lord's Prayer at least daily and preferably several times a day, giving careful thought to the meaning of each word or phrase.

Below is an adaptation of St. Ignatius' spiritual exercise on the Lord's Prayer. I learned the Lord's prayer as a child using the King James Version. There are more accurate modern translations but, in this exercise, I prefer the King James version (below), which Jesus gave us in the Sermon on the Mount.

> Our Father which art in heaven, Hallowed be thy name. Thy kingdom come, thy will be done in earth, as it is in heaven. Give us this day our daily bread. And forgive us our trespasses, as we forgive those who trespass against us. And lead us not into temptation but deliver us from evil:

For thine is the kingdom, and the power, and the glory, forever. Amen.... (Matt.6:6 – 13 KJV)

A SPIRITUAL EXERCISE ON THE LORD'S PRAYER

1. Set aside an hour for this exercise when and where you can be alone or at least undisturbed. Get rid of all distractions by turning off the TV and the phone.

2. Start by giving God the thanks for the opportunity to pray and to grow through this exercise. Ask God for the help of His Spirit to complete this exercise and to be blessed by it.

3. Take each work of the Lord's Prayer one at a time and carefully consider each word. For example the first word, "Our." Who is included in that word? All Christians? All who believe in God. All human beings? Which one do you think makes the most sense? The word "our" implies ownership; in what way is God yours? In what way is God every Christian's?

4. When you have thought of everything you can think of related to the word and considered your answers to the questions you raised, move on to the next word. "Father" In what way is God your father? As creator of the universe? As the father of the human race? As your actual father? How do you experience God as father? In what way is God father of all people? In what way is God the father of the church?

5. Think not just of these questions but any that come to your mind and think also of what your answer is to the questions would be.

6. Take your time and spend as much time with each word as you feel comfortable. There is no right or wrong amount of time, however:

7. Take no less than 45 minutes to complete the exercise and no more than 60 minutes – even if you are only a few words in.

8. End with a prayer to thank God for the insights you gained in the exercise.

Chapter Sixteen: The Balcony

Originally preached June 30, 2019

This book ends with a visit to the metaphorical balcony. The rest of the palace is built and now it time to go outside and enjoy the balcony.

Any palace I would want to own would have a large patio or balcony, from which I can admire the view, and on which I could hold parties. The balcony that comes to my mind for my spiritual palace is the beautiful balcony of the Ringling Museum in Sarasota that extends out over the water of Sarasota Bay. It is beautifully made of stone and tile and concrete; a balcony large enough to accommodate several hundred guests in a stunningly beautiful setting. The spiritual palace balcony I am talking about in this chapter is a metaphor for the three main things I would do on my balcony if I owned a palace with a balcony: just sit and relax, have parties on it; and take in the view from it daily.

Before we go on would you join me in prayer?

> Lord God, I thank You for what this book has meant to me. I have been surprised at the insights I have gotten from it and I have grown through it. May this chapter be more water on my spiritual roots and refreshing dew for my soul.

The Balcony Is Great for Relaxing

I saw a funny internet meme recently it said, "1. Going to bed early 2. Not leaving my house 3. Required naps. My childhood punishments are now my adult goals." I would add to that list of adult goals - having to take a day to sit around and do nothing important.

God who knows us intimately as our creator and Father knows of our needs, including our need for rest and relaxation. In Genesis (2:2) we read that God rested for a day following creation. If God wants a rest how much more do, we need rest and restoration for the journey?

Jesus described a difficult path or road that Christians are called to travel on (Matthew 7:13-14).

> You can enter God's Kingdom only through the narrow gate. The highway to hell is broad, and its gate is wide for the many who choose that way. 14But the gateway to life is very narrow and the road is difficult, and only a few ever find it.

As Christians we have all the usual burdens of the life of a non-believer – stay out of trouble, earn a living, take care of our responsibilities. As Christians we carry the additional burden of living a life that is pleasing to God. Jesus said, "Take my yoke upon you. Let me teach you, because I am humble and gentle at heart, and you will find rest for your souls. [30]For my yoke is easy to bear, and the burden I give you is light" (Matthew 11:29-30 NLT). His burden is the burden of living a blessed life. It is light and its rewards certainly outweigh its requirements, but it is an additional burden none-the-less.

Our journey on Jesus' path is a marathon not a sprint. In the safety lecture at the start of every airplane flight the cabin steward announces, "In case of emergency oxygen masks will drop from the ceiling, put your own mask on first and then help anyone else around you." In the same way we must not be shy about feeding our spirit and body with the things that renew us and give us joy so that we have the energy we need and are equipped to keep on keeping on. It is okay and we should not feel guilty that our times of rest and relaxation include more than just honoring the Sabbath day.

The Balcony Is Our Party Place

The balcony is also a metaphor for the places and times we set aside to party with others. Yes, a part of building a spiritual palace relationship with God involves partying (not in the slang term meaning using drugs), celebration, eating, drinking (not in a self-destructive way or in a way harmful to anyone else) and having a good time with others. One of the things that is easy to overlook, if you are not a biblical scholar or serious Bible student, is the fact that our God seems to really like a party. We see that implied in the story of the wedding at Cana where Jesus miraculously produced 6 very large containers of wine. We hear it repeated four times in Ecclesiastes – there is nothing better than eating and drinking and enjoying life. And we see it in the holidays that God commanded the people of Israel to observe.

If you are going to have a party, you need time off so you can have it, and God was pretty progressive in His labor laws. In the centuries and millenniums before labor laws, God required that we all have at least one day off a week, and He also mandated that we also have about the same number of paid holidays and vacation days per year as the average beginning worker gets in America today (2019)! In Deuteronomy 16 we read:

> "Three times a year all your males shall appear before the LORD your God at the place that he will choose: at the festival of unleavened bread, at the festival of weeks, and at the festival of booths." And "You shall keep the festival of booths for <u>seven days</u>… *you shall surely celebrate.*"

The commandment for all the men to appear includes all the women by default, and it is worth noting that *you shall surely celebrate* is a commandment that we celebrate! That is a commandment from God to party!

As Christians we don't observe any seven day long religious holidays like the festival of booths or Hanukah, but the intention of God behind the commandments, 'you *shall* keep these festivals, you *shall* celebrate" is still there. For several reasons God wants us to, and God has commanded us to, party. First, this is not just time off, this is time off in celebration of God, and at the command of God; thus our obedience reaffirms God's dominant place in our lives. Second, God loves us and wants us to be as happy as we can be in life, and there is a joy that comes to us in celebrating; even the most dour and introverted people come to life at a party or celebration. Third, God wants us joyful because our joyfulness is the best advertisement for relationship with God that there is. If you are a sourpuss you might be cynical about someone who is always joyful, and you might mock them, but secretly you want what they have. When I was in the Marine Corps, I heard a lot about the Marine esprit de corps; that is an attitude of self-confidence in the organization that Marines project because of their training and fitness. Christians project an attitude of self-confidence because of who we are (children of God) and who is within us (the Holy Spirit), and what we feel (the peace, love and joy of the Lord) inside us. People can see the joy and love on us, and they want it.

Lastly, God also wants us to celebrate our victories for God. When have done some self-reflection and you realize you have accomplished a goal you set out to accomplish in your relationship with God, then celebrate it! If you wanted to make a commitment to serve at least once a month and you realize you have done it; or if you have lost the weight that you pledged to God you would lose; or if you have been wanting for years to read the Bible every day, or to pray every day and you have finally made that a habit. Then celebrate your accomplishments, really celebrate it – buy something special for yourself; invite your family and friends to join you and honor your victory in Jesus whatever it is.

God wants us to be party people because it is done in obedience to God, because it keeps us going strong, and because our joyfulness through the Holy Spirit is attractive to others. Our celebrations are like gas stations along the highway of life, we fill up with joy through celebration as we go along, and it powers us through the drudgery and tough times.

The Balcony as A Place to Take in The View of Your Life

I love balconies, not just because I really enjoy admiring a beautiful view, but I love the self-reflection on life that time spent on balconies seem to lead to. When I am on a beautiful balcony looking out at an amazing view, seeing that great distance and slice of the beauty of God's creation, it helps me put myself in perspective. The view from a balcony can help us see more clearly how small we are compared to the magnitude of God's creation, and that humbling realization is a very important perspective to have in our relationship with God. If we are not humble before God, we don't have a real relationship with God (Psalm 18:27; James 4:6). The most profound humility comes from seeing our self-image reflected in the mirror of God or some part of God's creation.

I mentioned in Chapter Five that an examination of our conscience or our thoughts and behaviors is a part of our Biblical tradition and is essential to building up our relationship with God and in Chapter Fourteen I mentioned that it is a part of our spiritual maintenance. The owner of the spiritual palace has an ongoing job that is more than just building the structure: unlike an earthly palace a spiritual palace is not a permanent structure; its walls and foundation are a living structure that must be continually nourished by the strong power of God in the Holy Spirit. The free flow of the Spirit of God in our lives requires us to remove the barriers to that flow which a lack of humility puts up. In his 2nd Letter to the Corinthians Paul wrote: "Examine yourselves and find out if you really are true to your faith." We need to take time for self-reflection regularly if not daily.

One of the best and easiest ways to make time for self-reflection is through the daily use of the Lord's Prayer. As we pray, "Forgive us our trespasses as we forgive those who trespass against us", every time we pray that our thought ought to be, "how am I doing in forgiving others?" And when we pray, "lead us not into temptation but deliver us from evil", every time our thoughts ought to be "How am I doing in resisting temptation and evil?" Jesus taught us to pray that prayer with the implication being that we will pray it daily. That means Jesus realized that every day we will face the temptation to sin, and very likely we will not win every battle every day. So a daily examination of conscience is in order, at least to the extent of using the Lord's prayer for self-reflection.

Examination of conscience is most effective when we are able to visualize its findings; our mistakes are easier not to repeat if they are burned into our minds. I have not fought a boxing match in over 40 years, but I can still remember some of the key moments of key fights; both the great punches that I landed and those that landed on me. After each fight I went over it again and again in my mind, seeing those key moments clearly and holding the images up to questions like: "Did I bob when I should have weaved? Did I jab when I should have hooked?" How were my hands positioned when that punch came in?" The metaphor of the balcony as a place to see the view is about the big picture of your spiritual life – combining both the self-awareness and perhaps self-criticism of an examination of conscience with a vision of the future and what we want to see going forward, as we are growing into in our relationship with God.

The famous sculptor Michelangelo was asked the secret of how he could take a block of marble and turn it into a beautiful statue. His response was "I see what there within the stone and I remove everything that does not belong." Obviously, that is much easier said than done, but in a way, he is describing the process of building a spiritual palace. Our relationship with God is the block of stone; our vision is what we hope to see revealed in our lives; and our self-examination lets us see what still needs to be removed. And our spiritual task to be engaged in the process of chipping away gently and carefully over time to reveal more and more of the glory we are called to live and to be.

As a pastor I often get called on for counseling. People come in for counseling because they cannot get a handle an issue in their life or a question or concern that they have. As strange as it may seem, the person seeking counseling either cannot visualize or get a picture in their minds about their problem itself, or they cannot see a solution, or both. My process is simple, I listen to them vent at first; it is a relief for most people just to talk about their problem to someone; to start getting it out is the beginning of the healing process or of finding a solution. It used to surprise me how often I would ask a person "what is the problem, and why is it a problem for you?" And, they would reply "I am not sure." It sounds hard to believe that someone would come to counseling not sure what their problem is, but I find often times people come because they know something is wrong, or someone has told them you have a problem and they believe it but cannot see it for themselves. A wise professor taught me that most of the time, on some level people know what the solution to their problem is and your job as counselor is help them see what is already inside them.

So, I try to draw them out bit by bit until the picture emerges. Quite often they are confused because they have many problems wrapped up in the one larger presenting symptom that brought them into counseling. "I don't know why my wife is angry at me all the time" might be the presenting problem, but there are generally multiple problems wrapped up in that one issue. By reflecting back to them what I have heard I eventually enable them to get a visual image of what they are going through. I find that just to have a visual image of what they are going through is an immediate help, and often it is the key to unlocking their puzzle. Quite often when they can see their problems clearly the solution also quickly becomes visible.

The process of examination of conscience can take the place of a counselor for helping us see what our spiritual problems are, (but having a trustworthy spiritual advisor is also a good idea) and our vision is about fixing those problems and moving past them to the future we want.

As a tool for self-reflection I have put together a diagram that shows the different components of building and maintaining a spiritual palace relationship with God that I have lifted up in the book. Take a look at the diagram before you go and think about how you are doing in each of these areas and where your most significant growth need is – that is to say where you are the weakest. Below the diagram is a description of the steps you can use in the process of self-evaluation as you take in the view from your balcony to look at the components of your spiritual life.

Stop & Reflect:

Of course we need to find time and a place for self-reflection; ideally setting aside one thirty-sixty-minute space is best, but unlike some of the other spiritual exercises this type of reflection can be done in ten-minute segments as time and life allows. As always, we begin with prayer, asking God for wisdom and insight to see things from God's perspective, for patience and openness to hear and see what God may want you to see, and for inspiration from the Spirit to strengthen the desire to carry it all through. We end this prayer with a full minute or even two to just listen in silence to feel the presence of God and to hear any reply or message from God, and we thank God for His help.

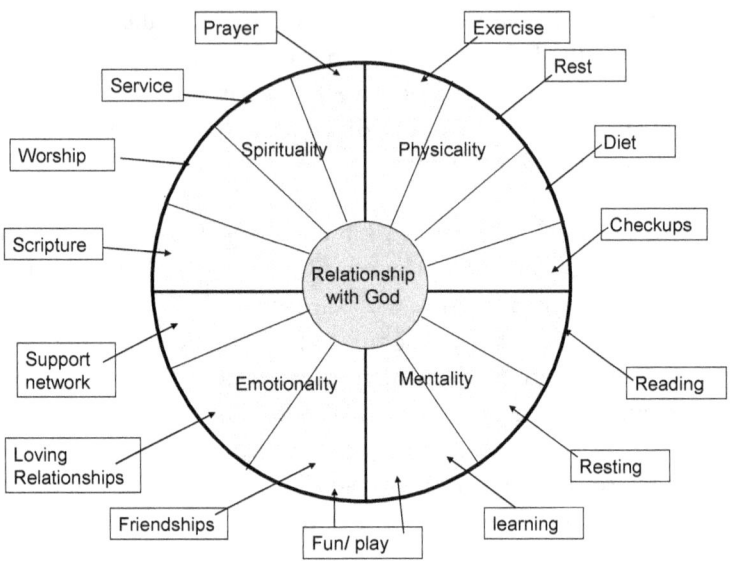

Foundation & Building Blocks

At the center of the wheel is our relationship with God. Around it are the four main areas of health – physical, mental, emotional and spiritual, and the main contributing elements of health for each. So one by one consider each of the eleven different foundational elements, evaluate the progress you've made, and the things you still need to change or improve. Each of the eleven items surrounding wheel is mentioned in one or more chapters of this book, with enough information about it to facilitate an adequate time of self-reflection.

The most essential thing we want to accomplish in our self-reflection is to ask ourselves how we are doing at obeying the law of love. At the center of the diagram relationship with God has at its core loving God. A spiritual palace relationship with God is about loving God, truly loving God with all of our heart mind soul and strength and truly obeying his commandments that we love others and that we love ourselves. The Apostle Paul wrote to the Romans: 'The commandments, "You shall not commit adultery; You shall not murder; You shall not steal; You shall not covet"; and any other commandment, are summed up in this word, "Love your neighbor as yourself.'" He was paraphrasing what Jesus said, "The entire law and all the demands of the prophets are based on these two commandments" (the two commandments being to love God with all of our heart, mind, soul, and strength, and our neighbors as ourselves). Everything in this book can also be accomplished if you could perfectly love God, love your neighbor and love yourself.

Albert Schweitzer was a doctor, a theologian, an author, a medical missionary and a winner of the Nobel Peace Prize. His most famous teaching was "the reverence for life" the philosophy that 'no person must ever harm or destroy life unless absolutely necessary.' My granddad, who was also a German doctor and musician, was very much influenced by Schweitzer. Schweitzer wrote: "What we call *love* is in its essence reverence for life." My granddad turned that around to say reverence for life is another way to say love, and my Granddad's philosophy was: *"you shall take no action towards others not taken in love, with love, and for love."* I think that is another way to sum up Jesus' teachings and it gives us another way to reflect on our level of compliance with those two most challenging commandments of Jesus.

The final part of our reflection is to identify the weakness that have been holding us back in any of these areas and lift them up to God asking God to heal you or strengthen you where help is needed. Self-examination and reflection are about looking at the past. Lastly, we want to look ahead to the future – to renew our vision. How do you want your relationship with God to be different in the future from what it is now? Has your reflection pointed you in a new direction that you want to grow in, to expand your knowledge of God and/or your experience of God and/or your love for God? End the exercise by telling God in prayer where you would like to be in your relationship with God

in the future and confirm to God that will devote yourself to carrying out these changes. Lastly, if you journal, record your intentions in your journal. **Scripture Quotes: The Law of Love**
Preached June 30, 2019

2 Corinthians 13:5-6 (CEV) Test yourselves and find out if you really are true to your faith. If you pass the test, you will discover that Christ is living in you. But if Christ isn't living in you, you have failed. ⁶I hope you will discover that we have not failed.

Exodus 20:8-11 (TEV) 8 "Observe the Sabbath and keep it holy. 9 You have six days in which to do your work, 10but the seventh day is a day of rest dedicated to me. On that day no one is to work—neither you, your children, your slaves, your animals, nor the foreigners who live in your country.

Matthew 22:35-40 (NLT) 35One of them, an expert in religious law, tried to trap him with this question: 36"Teacher, which is the most important commandment in the law of Moses? "Jesus replied, "'You must love the LORD your God with all your heart, all your soul, and all your mind.' 38This is the first and greatest commandment. 39A second is equally important: 'Love your neighbor as yourself.' 40The entire law and all the demands of the prophets are based on these two commandments."

Romans 13:9-10 (NRSV) 9The commandments, "You shall not commit adultery; You shall not murder; You shall not steal; You shall not covet"; and any other commandment, are summed up in this word, "Love your neighbor as yourself." 10Love does no wrong to a neighbor; therefore, love is the fulfilling of the law.

Deuteronomy 16:13-15 Rejoice during your festival, you and your sons and your daughters, your male and female slaves, as well as the Levites, the strangers, the orphans, and the widow's resident in your towns. ¹⁵Seven days you shall keep the festival to the LORD your God at the place that the LORD will choose; for the LORD your God will bless you in all your produce and in all your undertakings, and <u>you shall surely celebrate</u>.16Three times a year <u>all your males shall appear before the LORD your God at the place that he will choose: at the festival of unleavened bread, at the festival of weeks, and at the festival of booths</u>. They shall not appear before the LORD empty-handed

Matthew 6:24-25, 32-33 (NLT) 24"No one can serve two masters. For you will hate one and love the other; you will be devoted to one and despise the other. <u>You cannot serve both God and money</u>. "That is why I tell you n<u>ot to worry about everyday life—whether you have enough food and drink, or enough clothes to wear</u>. Isn't life more than food, and your body more than clothing? 32These things dominate the thoughts of unbelievers, but your heavenly Father already knows all your needs. 33<u>Seek the Kingdom of God above all else, and live righteously, and he will give you everything you need</u>.

Isaiah 2:4 The LORD will mediate between nations and will settle international disputes. They will hammer their swords into plowshares and their spears into pruning hooks. Nation will no longer fight against nation, nor train for war anymore.

Genesis 2:2 On the seventh day God had finished his work of creation, so he rested from all his work.

Matthew 7:13-14 "You can enter God's Kingdom only through the narrow gate. The highway to hell is broad, and its gate is wide for the many who choose that way. 14But the gateway to life is very narrow and the road is difficult, and only a few ever find it.

1 Chronicles 29:11-12 Yours, O LORD, is the greatness, the power, the glory, the victory, and the majesty. Everything in the heavens and on earth is yours, O LORD, and this is your kingdom. We adore you as the one who is over all things. ^{12}Wealth and honor come from you alone, for you rule over everything. Power and might are in your hand, and at your discretion people are made great and given strength.

1 John 4:8 But anyone who does not love does not know God, for God is love.

1 Thessalonians 1:4 We know, dear brothers and sisters, that God loves you and has chosen you to be his own people.

John 3:16 "For God loved the world so much that he gave his one and only Son, so that everyone who believes in him will not perish but have eternal life.

Matthew 7:24-27 "Anyone who listens to my teaching and follows it is wise, like a person who builds a house on solid rock. ^{25}Though the rain comes in torrents and the floodwaters rise and the winds beat against that house, it won't collapse because it is built on bedrock. ^{26}But anyone who hears my teaching and ignores it is foolish, like a person who builds a house on sand. ^{27}When the rains and floods come, and the winds beat against that house, it will collapse with a mighty crash."

A Spiritual Exercise for Reflection, Vision and Commitment

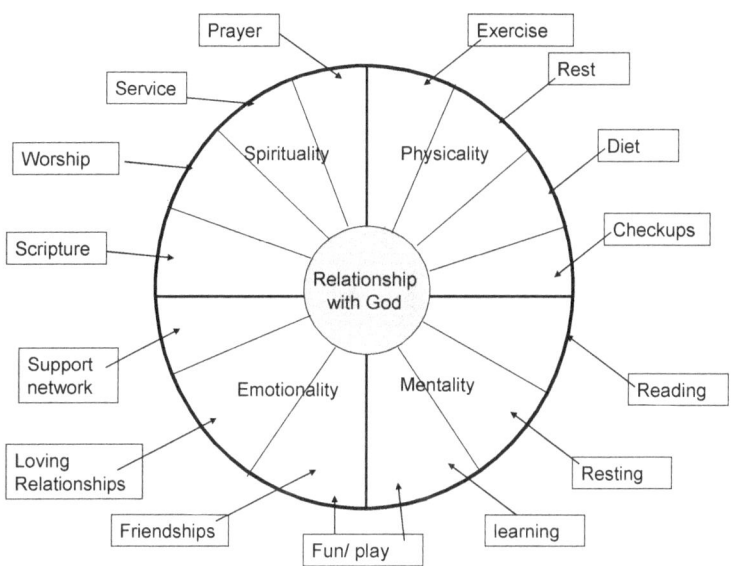

The Basic Elements of a Spiritual Palace
The Process of Self Reflection

STOP: Take a seat "on the balcony"

LISTEN: Pray for guidance; and listen to the leadership and wisdom of the Holy Spirit to help you

IDENTIFY: Taking each point one at a time, starting with the center, and ask yourself these questions:

1. Can I honestly say I love God with all of my heart mind, soul and strength? If not where am I weak and why, and what can I do to improve?

2. Do my actions reflect that I love my neighbor as myself?

3. Do my actions reflect that I love myself as much as I love my neighbor?

4. Am I doing the basic things I need to be doing to take care of my overall healthiness in this area that is foundational for spiritual growth?

5. Am I using my unique gifts, skills, passions, strengths or talents in this area? If not, what can I do to improve?

6. What progress have I made since I began, and what weaknesses, sins or blind spots have I identified that are holding me back?

7. What progress do I want to have made in the next 5 years?

8. Pray and give God thanks for any insights gained and commit to God any changes that you have identified.

9. Record your insights and commitments to God in a journal.

ACT: celebrate your victories; make a plan and a timeline goal for the needs identified.

EPILOGUE

As any teacher will tell you, every time you set out to teach you also learn in the process, and I certainly learned as I was writing. My own spiritual palace is continually being built up and maintained. I trust that God who loves you and wants what is best for you has also used this book to guide you to think about the wonder that God's desire for you is to take on the light burden of the work of discipleship so that you have truly the most enjoyable and abundant life it is possible for you to live. What a wonder and a joy it is that our best possible life comes to us through our relationship with God the Father, through Christ the Son, in the fullness of the Holy Spirit.

Each chapter of this book started out as a sermon, and the writing of each sermon started with and was bathed in prayer. Every time I sat down to work on writing this book, I began with an extensive prayer time. Through prayer we avail ourselves of the rich blessings that come to us in a close personal relationship with God. As Christians our prayers for one another have tremendous impact. Jesus stands at the door of our lives knocking and prayer is how we open the door and invite him in.

I want to invite you to join me in one last prayer together:

A COVENANT PRAYER

> Lord, I covenant with you to give you my best; my best effort, my best offerings. I commit to you that I will offer you my body, my mind, my soul, all I am, and all I have every day. As long as I have breath I will seek. I will seek to know you; I will seek to love you completely; I will seek to be worthy of you; I will seek to be worthy of all you have blessed me with; and I will seek to live in to and up to all that you are calling me to be and to accomplish for you.

Fill me with your Holy Spirit I pray to strengthen me for this task and empower me for the long haul. You are my shepherd and I am one of your flock; protect me and guide me for your name's sake. All glory, honor, praise, joy, love and thanks to you Father, Son and Holy Spirit, now and forever! Amen.

Please feel free to contact me: write to me at my church address:

13400 Park Blvd.

Seminole, Fl. 33776

www.ingramcontent.com/pod-product-compliance
Lightning Source LLC
Chambersburg PA
CBHW071324110526
44591CB00010B/1018